The
Inspiration
Factor

HOW YOU CAN REVITALIZE YOUR
COMPANY CULTURE IN **12** WEEKS

Terry Barber

WITH PAT SPRINGLE

GREENLEAF
BOOK GROUP PRESS

Published by Greenleaf Book Group Press, Austin, TX, www.gbgpress.com

Distributed by Greenleaf Book Group LLC

For ordering information or special discounts for bulk purchases, please contact Greenleaf Book Group LLC at PO Box 91869, Austin, TX 78709, 512.891.6100.

Design and composition by Greenleaf Book Group LLC
Cover design by Greenleaf Book Group LLC

Publisher's Cataloging-in-Publication Data (Prepared by The Donohue Group, Inc.)

Barber, Terry (Terry Ray), 1955-
  The inspiration factor : how you can revitalize your company culture in 12 weeks /
Terry Barber ; with Pat Springle. -- 2nd ed.

   p. ; cm.

  ISBN: 978-1-60832-026-4

1. Motivation (Psychology)--Popular works. 2. Intergroup relations--Popular works.
3. Inspiration. 4. Corporate culture. I. Springle, Pat, 1950- II. Title.

BF503 .B37 2010
153.8   2009937563

Part of the Tree Neutral™ program, which offsets the number of trees consumed in the production and printing of this book by taking proactive steps, such as planting trees in direct proportion to the number of trees used: www.treeneutral.com

TreeNeutral

Printed in the United States of America on acid-free paper

09 10 11 12 13 14   10 9 8 7 6 5 4 3 2 1

Second Edition

Teach . . . and hopefully they will learn.
Lead . . . and they may follow.
Inspire . . . and they will never be the same.

CONTENTS

FOREWORD

"CULTURE TRUMPS STRATEGY." This simple statement, made by the CEO of a billion-dollar organization that I was coaching, has stayed with me for years. No matter what brilliant plans you may have for your team or organization, or even your family, if there is not a culture of authenticity and loyalty, those plans will never materialize.

Terry Barber is one of those rare people who are a force of nature. His exuberance for life and genuine love for people belie a brilliant strategic mind that has been honed in one of the toughest markets there is: raising money for youth organizations. Now he has expanded that into various moneymaking enterprises, all without losing his soul.

Simply put, if Terry believes in something, everyone around him eventually will too. What excites me about this book is that someone has taken a natural gifting of inspiration and enthusiasm and broken it down into parts that other people can learn to emulate.

Whether it is learning to be true to oneself, which is the beginning of authenticity, or learning to appreciate and value the benefits of great storytelling, this book brings it all together in simple, easy-to-understand language, filled with real-life examples.

I hope you have the pleasure of meeting Terry Barber one day. Once you get in his orbit you yourself begin to spin a little faster, believe in yourself a little more, see the sunshine instead of the shadow, and laugh your deepest laugh.

If you don't ever meet Terry personally, the very least you can do is buy this book and read it. It is like liquid nitrogen on paper—shake it up in your own life and watch your results explode into joy and delight and beauty.

I call him "T-Ray" for a reason. He is bigger than life.

Read this work, and you will be too.

Laurie Beth Jones
Author of *The Path; Jesus CEO;* and *Jesus, Life Coach*

ACKNOWLEDGMENTS

MY LIFE IS FULL of passion and contentment mostly because it contains a rich portfolio of relationships. To the people with whom I "do life," I owe much gratitude.

To my daughters—Brittany, Lindsey, Tommee, and Amanda—thank you for giving me the freedom to speak the principles in this book into your lives. In the process, I actually learned more than I taught.

To my mom and dad, thank you for inspiring me to pursue dreams that require my God-given unique gifts and talents. You never gave up on me.

To my three little sisters and younger brother. You at least acted interested when, at the age of ten, I tried out new speeches on you as an aspiring public speaker—thanks, guys. I'm more than grateful.

I'm also very grateful for people who loved me enough to speak the hard truth. One such individual is my good friend Laurie Beth Jones. After a day of whining to her about what a victim I was of some difficult times, she quickly reminded me of the truth about who I was. Immediately, I stopped playing the role of a victim. Laurie Beth, thank you for the pep talk!

To Pat Springle, who helped move an idea for a book to the reality of this book, I'm very thankful. I appreciate your diligence, your partnership, and above all, your friendship. My life is truly richer because of you.

To my good friend Larry Bone—you and I have been doing life together for thirty-seven years. As my youth leader in 1971, you saw potential in me that I certainly didn't see in myself. All your life, Larry, you have pursued a vision much bigger than yourself. You have enjoyed the friendship of many people, but your greatest reward will come when heaven reveals the untold numbers of people, like me, that you have inspired.

My life has been molded and catapulted by several other inspiring people. Four of them are my longtime friends Jerry Riggs, Scott Kimbro, Jamie Wright, and Duncan Dodds. Jerry, I'm grateful that God put you into my life. Scott, thank you for always reminding me that all things do work together for good. Jamie, your enthusiasm is contagious, and I am a better person because of you. And thank you, Duncan, for believing in me even when I found it hard to believe in myself.

One of the blessings of my job is that I've been able to watch some of my clients create inspiring cultures in their companies and organizations. I thank each of them for their example: Cindy Eller, Laurel Dibrog, and Candace Johnson have done a masterful job at the Roswell Park Cancer Institute in Buffalo, New York. Paola Werstler and Scott Thompson have worked to inspire their team at the Arizona Cancer Center. I've also seen the powerfully positive impact of Rosemary Gruber and her husband, Don, at the University of Minnesota Cancer Center; and Carol Jefferson and her husband, David, at the Holden Cancer Center at the University of Iowa. Finally, Jon Huntsman and his team at the Huntsman Cancer Institute inspire me every time I'm around them, especially my friend and client Heather Levan. I love these people.

I also want to say a special thank-you to Chip Grizzard and my coworkers at Grizzard Communications Group, Inc., who have given me the opportunity to put into practice the life-enhancing principles contained in this book. What a privilege it is to work for a company with such a high standard of integrity.

Several people have influenced me profoundly, though I have never met them in person. It's the words they put into print that have inspired me. Every year for the past twenty years I've read Dale Carnegie's classic book *How to Win Friends and Influence People*. A few years ago, C. S. Lewis challenged me in his book *The Problem of Pain* with the thought that pain is "God's megaphone" to get our attention. It was Lewis's authentic approach to pain that first allowed me to turn the most difficult time of my life into a defining moment.

To my publishing partners at Greenleaf Book Group, especially Bill Crawford, who continued to push me for more personal stories, thank you. For the ongoing encouragement and editing of Renee Chavez, thank you.

Finally, I want to say thank you to my wife, Debbi, who never grows tired of seeing the best in me. Debbi, you too have created an inspirational culture—at work and in our home. I'm indebted to you.

Redefining Inspiration

Keep away from people who try to belittle your ambitions. Small people always do that, but the really great make you feel that you, too, can become great.
—Mark Twain, American author, humorist, satirist

IF I WERE TO ASK YOU to come up with some synonyms for the word *inspiration*, what would you tell me? *Stimulation*, no doubt—in the sense of exciting and uplifting your emotions. Or *encouragement*—in the sense of people influencing others. *Brainstorm* is popular too—in the sense of creative ideas. The number one answer I hear, though, is *motivation*. Most folks say motivation and inspiration are one and the same.

Over the years, however, I've seen a sometimes subtle but often significant distinction between motivation and inspiration. Motivation provides an incentive for people to act in certain ways, but for reasons that can be noble . . . *or* selfish. They may even act out of fear. *Motivation*, therefore, can either be positive or negative, productive or destructive.

Inspiration, on the other hand, is always good, always positive. It focuses on people's deepest and noblest desires. According to *Merriam-Webster's*

Collegiate Dictionary (eleventh edition), to *inspire* is, in fact, to exert an "exalting influence."

Definitions matter.

Most business books and seminars focus on motivation, and they often encourage executives and managers to use the full range of incentives to motivate employees along the corporate ladder. Sometimes, these leaders succeed. They take those "motivational principles" back to the workplace, and their employees do, indeed, become motivated. Management and staff are doing an outstanding job.

Most of the time, however, leaders motivate their people through manipulation, fear, and threats, and the consequences can be devastating rather than encouraging. In these cases, motivation is short-lived because these leaders only scratched the surface of their people's potential.

Motivation vs. Inspiration: A Case in Point

My relationship with my father taught me a lot about the differences between motivation and inspiration. When I was a boy, Dad used three forms of inducement with me: positive motivation, manipulative motivation, and inspiration. Two of these were counterproductive.

More times than I care to remember, when I brought my report card home from school, my father would study it, give me one of those looks that said it all, sigh deeply, and say: "Son, this just won't do. You're living *way below* your potential. You've got to figure out a way to apply yourself and do better—a *lot* better." Positive motivation. And my father meant well with his "do better" speech, but this method of motivation never produced long-term positive change.

Still, it would work for a time, because his positive motivation was often backed with manipulative motivation, namely, a threat, spoken or not. I was well aware that if I didn't do better in the next term, I'd experience severe consequences. I had five siblings—two brothers and three sisters—and Dad had no favorites. We were all very familiar with what we referred to simply as "the belt." Fear is a powerful motivator, but it's a lousy source of inspiration. (I'm not claiming, by the way, that I didn't deserve the belt from time to time. I'm just explaining that, while it definitely "motivated" me and manipulated me to enhance my performance, it certainly didn't *inspire* me.)

On many mornings, Dad's attitude and actions inspired me. He would stand in the kitchen, making his coffee, singing and clapping to the rhythm of Tennessee Ernie Ford. Then, as he drove me to school, he would ask me questions such as, "Son, what are you looking forward to today?" and "How are you going to make a difference today?" These questions, and the smile on his face as he asked them, made me want to be like him—*inspired* me to be like him. They also assured me that my father believed in me—and I ate it up! Those times with my father made me a better man.

An example of true inspiration occurred the day Dad took me to work with him. At the time, his customers were lumberyard owners and managers. I'll always remember him introducing me to each and every one, all through the day. He taught me to shake hands assertively, with a good, firm grip. He told me to look his customers in the eye and say my name loud and clear. I remember thinking: *I want to be able to meet people like my dad does. I'd love to have people like me as much as they like him.*

Dad did more that day than just motivate me for a brief period of time. He actually tapped into my dreams (to impact people) and gave me a vision, not just for that day but for my future as well. In fact, *every* time my father inspired me, he had a powerful effect on me. That's how inspiration works, and that's the difference between it and motivation. Leaders who genuinely *inspire* others do so by tapping into people's dreams, eliciting the best from them, and ultimately, changing their lives. Perhaps these leaders have an intuitive knack for inspiring those around them—or they may have developed this skill through years of training and trial and error, as my father did. Either way, it is the *inspiration factor* that produces more positive transformations than any other leadership trait.

> Leaders who genuinely *inspire* others do so by tapping into people's dreams, eliciting the best from them, and ultimately, changing their lives.

Lessons Learned—The Hard Way

Many years after that day at Dad's workplace—with college, graduate school, and several years of work behind me—I was asked to supervise a group of interns for a year. I was thirty-one, and it was my first management role. I'd taken courses in management, I'd read books about business, and I'd had countless conversations about the best ways to lead, manage, and motivate people. But when my first four interns walked through the door, I reverted to the "live up to your potential" kind of motivation that my father had used with me. I had learned to use positive words—but in a negative, threatening way: "Live up to your potential . . . *or you'll have to answer for it!*"

As the months went by, some patterns surfaced. Sometimes my interns worked really hard, but often I could tell that their hearts just weren't in it. From time to time, their minds would drift from the tasks assigned to them, and a couple of them were habitually late for meetings. Almost every day, I kicked into my corrective mode, chiding with sayings like these:

- What's the problem? Let me see your daily planner. You've got to maximize your day!

- Repeat after me, with enthusiasm: *"We are fired up. We love our work. We are world changers!"*

- We've got work to do! Our mission is much more important than we are, and we have the chance to *make a difference!*

- If you don't get going, there are other people right behind you who are waiting to take your job.

- I need you to be here on time—and the second you get here, you'd better be fired up!

To be honest, they responded to me exactly as I had responded to my father's live-up-to-your-potential talk. Each time I met with one of them concerning personal performance, he or she would do better—for a day or two—but then revert to old habits.

As the director of a youth outreach program, I came to manage several groups of interns. My vision was to have an intern in twenty-five of the largest high schools in Houston, Texas, each of whom would provide leadership training. Invariably, in every group, one of the interns would do everything I asked—with a smile on his or her face! Soon it dawned on me why teachers have "pets" in their classes; I had them too! My delight in my favorites caused even more conflict in my relationships with those who, I was sure, needed a "butt-kicking" every few days.

My experience overseeing the interns was both exhilarating and frustrating. When they responded to me, I saw the light in their eyes because they connected their talents and ambitions with a transcendent purpose, and I was thrilled! But the reasons they gave for their failures and their whining about every imaginable thing just about drove me crazy. It seemed that the more I endeavored to inspire them, the more they made excuses for their behavior. I tried all kinds of motivational techniques, but nothing seemed to work. I wanted their hearts to be captured by the vision of making a difference so that nothing else mattered. A few got it, but many didn't. I kept trying to pump them up, but they leaked—really badly. I felt like a colossal failure.

My frustration drove me to look for answers, some of which I found in a new book that had just hit the market: *The 7 Habits of Highly Effective People* by Stephen R. Covey. As I read it, one particular directive stood out as if it were written in neon lights: "Seek first to understand, then to be understood." I realized that the approach I had taken with the interns had been far too external. I had tried to pressure them into meeting my goals. I had failed miserably to touch their hearts. Gradually, I started to make changes in how I related to them.

One of the interns who drove me crazy was Ben, a laid-back, easygoing young man from Fort Worth, Texas. Over and over again, I tried to get him to do better by pointing out his flaws and telling him he was performing below his potential. After a while (and I suspect it didn't take long), he dreaded to see me coming. Armed with my new insight about inspiration, I took a different approach. I sat down with Ben and asked him about his goals, his dreams, and his ambitions. I invited dialogue and discovery: "Ben, tell me what attracted you to this intern position." Understandably, he seemed a bit hesitant at first, but soon, out of his mouth spilled clearly articulated dreams and aspirations—none of which I ever knew existed.

"Terry," he confided, "I've always been a little bashful, and I hoped this role would help me become more courageous and confident in connecting with people." That single statement melted my heart. It showed me how off target I had been in trying to shape Ben's life. In an instant, my thinking, my assumptions, and my process of relating to Ben changed. I knew I could genuinely inspire him by tying our projects to his personal goals.

With a new vision for my role as a manager, I met with my other interns. Each of them shared their dreams and desires, and I learned that each one had come to the program for very different reasons. Now I could tailor my interactions with each of them to tap into their unique, internal engines of motivation—and it made all the difference in the world!

Today, more than twenty years later, Ben tells people that I played an important role in his life. I can't tell you what that means to me, especially because I had failed so profoundly early in my relationship with him.

Ben wasn't the only one who was transformed by that experience, however. I had envisioned my role as the Master Disciplinarian whose task it was to force people to work hard, and with enthusiasm. Applying the maxim "Seek first to understand, then to be understood," I realized that my task was to connect the interns' hearts to the mission, to uncover their desires, to nurture their dreams, and to find the best way for them to fulfill those dreams within the organization.

Frankly, there wasn't always a good match between an intern's dreams and the organization's mission. As my perception of my role changed, my goal wasn't to force square pegs into round holes. Instead, I tried to find the best fit for people, and we celebrated when they found a new place where they could thrive, even if it meant they should work for a different employer.

Since those days, I've supervised many interns and overseen scores of direct and indirect reports both in business and in the nonprofit world. I certainly can't say that every single one of them adores me, but I have had the privilege of hearing from many of them that I was a source of inspiration and encouragement, and many have told me that I made a huge difference in the direction of their lives.

"Inspiration Begins at Home"

The insights I learned with my interns and the new direction I adopted for managing people had a compelling effect on my relationship with the three daughters I had at that time. (Daughter number four came along a few years later and benefited from my insights, I hope.) When they were youngsters—before the lights came on for me—I gave them the live-up-to-your-potential treatment that I had given to the interns, with very similar results. If you ask Brittany (the oldest of the three) about my parenting style when she, Lindsey, and Tommee were little girls, she would tell you that every week I demanded that they write their goals and post them on the refrigerator. (Try to picture that scene when they were seven, five, and three years old.) Then I'd review their goals and hold them accountable. I cringe when I think about my behavior, though they seemed to have gotten through it without too much damage. They tease me about it now—regularly.

When I began changing my corporate management style, I made the transition at home too. I started asking the girls about their hopes and dreams, and I delighted in their heartfelt motivation to achieve their own goals, not just to comply with mine. Today, my relationship with them is far different from what it would have been if I hadn't learned those lessons, and I am very, very grateful. They know that no one is more committed to their personal goals and dreams than I am. And that inspires them.

The Definition of Inspiration

Before we get very far, I want to be sure that we redefine the word *inspiration* to reflect the distinction between it and motivation. Too often, inspiration is seen merely as an *act*, and one that is merely fluff, at that—cheerleading devoid of substance, in other words—but in these pages, you'll see that inspiration is a *character trait*, an invaluable leadership characteristic that includes insights, skills, humility, and courage. It's not enough to pat people on the back occasionally and say, "You're great!" or "That's awesome!" Even though we may repeat it over and over, in essence that's a onetime act. We can do better than that—*much* better.

Inspiration is the developed *ability* and *commitment* to connect people's deepest motivations with their sharpest skills. When we inspire those around us, we develop strong relationships based on loyalty, not on manipulation or threats. Creating this kind of culture takes intention and effort, but it's worth it to see people thrive.

> Inspiration is a *character trait*, an invaluable leadership characteristic that includes insights, skills, humility, and courage . . . [as well as] the developed *ability* and *commitment* to connect people's deepest motivations with their sharpest skills.

In his insightful book *Good to Great*, author and professor Jim Collins writes that the greatest leaders build "enduring greatness [in the organization] through a paradoxical blend of personal humility and professional will."

Ego, drive, and charisma cause many leaders to focus only on their own goals instead of the dreams of others. Humility triggers the best leaders to look beyond themselves and care passionately about others around the office. Such behavior is an essential quality of leaders who inspire.

Collins was talking, of course, about top executives in major companies. But the same "paradoxical blend" can be developed in leaders at *any* level: in companies, nonprofit organizations, churches—and families. All of us bring particular abilities to our reporting relationships, and we can all learn to inspire people. It may be easier for some than others, but everyone can learn what I learned and have the kind of influence on others that I had on Ben, my children, and many others—as long as we keep our definitions straight.

INSPIRATION AND "WINDSPIRATION"

Too often, leaders do not have the humility they need to help others succeed—they are too focused on their own stellar reputations. All of us have worked under a leader such as this at one time or another.

Not long after completing my graduate degree, for instance, I went to work for a woman who was known as one of the nation's most respected leaders. She communicated a compelling vision with plenty of emotion. In fact, she was one of the most gifted speakers I've ever heard: her messages were colorful, challenging, and entertaining. Because of her reputation, I was certain she could mentor me, and I was equally certain that, under her leadership, I would become a comparably powerful leader and speaker.

Soon, however, my illusions were shattered. The more time I spent with her, the more I found out that she was all fluff, no substance. In other words, she was full of "windspiration," not inspiration. In fact, those who spent too much time with her were actually *drained* of inspiration. Why? Because she didn't care about the people who worked for her. This nationally known leader was so poor at understanding and inspiring people that she had to acquire new team and board members every few years. Each previous group left when they realized that she was an empty shell who did not—or perhaps could not—cultivate a real relationship with anyone.

Throughout my career, I've been around a number of leaders who offered nice platitudes but didn't take the time to get to know me and find out what drives me. Consequently, they didn't make much of a dent in my life. But I've also had the privilege of knowing—and being known by—a few wonderful leaders whose ability to inspire me changed my life.

When I was a bashful, awkward, annoying teenager living in New Orleans, my church youth worker was a young man named Larry Bone. As I think back on that time in my life, it's hard to imagine that Larry saw anything worth affirming in me, but he did. I distinctly remember one particular conversation when he looked me in the eye and said, "Terry, I can see that you really care about people and that you want to make a difference in their lives." Wow! That desire was certainly there, but it was buried deep in the muck of my adolescent insecurities. Larry wasn't through with his observations. He continued, "I think you have the potential to be a terrific communicator."

Me? I wondered as I looked around. *Is he talking to somebody else?*

No, he was talking to me. He saw latent abilities that I'd never dreamed were there.

One day Larry took me aside and told me solemnly: "Terry, there's more to life than you're living now. God has something for you that's much bigger than anything you've ever dreamed possible, and I believe you're going to achieve it. Do you want me to help you find out what it is?"

I jumped at his offer. "You bet I do!"

In my relationship with Larry, he never made me feel like a reclamation project. Even when I seemed to have very little to offer (which, looking back, was all day, every day), he treated me with respect. And Larry was the picture of humility. He never tried to be someone he wasn't. He often laughed and said, "I'm just a country boy from Arkansas" as he gave everything he had to every person around him.

Recently I told a friend about Larry's impact on me. "When was the last time you talked to him?" he asked. I had actually spoken with Larry the previous week. Through all these decades, marriages, children, jobs, and the other ups and downs in life we've remained great friends. People like Larry make that possible.

Whether he realized it or not, Larry successfully applied the very principles of inspiration that you will examine in the remainder of this book. As a result, he forged a genuine, lifelong relationship with me, and I will always be his loyal friend.

Whether your focus is on customers, clients, donors, employees, family, or friends, the principles of inspiration produce a deep, long-lasting sense of loyalty. In our fast-paced, fragmented, often shallow society, people long for authentic relationships that go below the surface and draw out their hidden or neglected dreams. Building these relationships is our biggest challenge and our highest privilege. It can be done, and it begins with examining our priorities.

Priorities

Whether we realize it or not, we organize our lives around just a few important relationships. Why? Because only a few people truly capture our hearts and shape our schedules. It is precisely these people whom we can—and should—seek to inspire, spending a disproportionate part of our emotional capital on them, and them alone. From time to time we may get out of balance and try to spread ourselves too thin. On these occasions, we need to change course and reset our priorities. It's not our job to inspire everybody everywhere.

So, who merits our concentrated investment? At the center of the target are our immediate families, our closest friends, and those who report to us at work—in that order. Every now and then we may carve out some time to devote attention to acquaintances or even passersby, but in so doing we'd better not neglect the people in the center. They deserve our prime hours, our best efforts, and our utmost care.

The next circle of people includes our extended families, coworkers, casual friends, and customers. We don't have as much emotional capital and time to invest in them as we do with our core circle, but if we're not careful, we can allow them to absorb too much of us, leaving us empty for the people in the center.

On the outermost circle are people we pass each day at work and on the street. They have few claims on our attention. That doesn't mean they aren't important; it just means we recognize that we have but a given amount of time and love to offer others, and we have decided to invest wisely in the innermost circles. Occasionally, we reach out to those whom Jesus called "the least of these" (Matthew 25:40), that is, the disadvantaged and downcast, but it is those in our *inner* circle whom we care for and provide an example to follow. As we intentionally make a difference in their lives, the ripple effect will probably touch those in the second circle and perhaps even the third. But if we are never specific and purposeful about those we most want to inspire, time will fly by, and we will have made little positive impact.

The Bottom Line

Corporate executives are always mindful of the bottom line, which consists of both tangibles and intangibles. With regard to inspiration, the most significant entry on the intangible side is the spirit of the employees, which has a direct bearing on the tangible assets. If you don't believe it, consider this: many of the companies on *Fortune*'s list of "100 Best Companies to Work For" are also some of the best performers on the stock markets. And though this is not a book about business growth, I do want to point out the direct correlation between a company's inspiration factor and its market value. Inspiring organizations not only make more money but also have better employee retention and higher degrees of customer loyalty than their competitors.

In their book *The Value Profit Chain*, James Heskett, Earl Sasser, and Leonard Schlesinger define the "Profit Chain Proposition" as people, process, and profit. That doesn't mean profits aren't important, but profits come more readily when inspired, confident, competent, enthusiastic employees connect with one another in a desire to create inspiring experiences for their customers. Companies that operate by the Profit Chain Proposition are some of the most profitable and, I believe, the most inspiring brands in the world: Southwest Airlines, International Paper, Ritz-Carlton, and Chick-fil-A, to name but a few. Their managers produce a wealth of intangible capital because they have learned the art and science of inspiring their employees, who in turn inspire their customers.

Similarly, parents who inspire their children not only enjoy deep and meaningful relationships with them but also build value into their lives—increasing each child's "bottom line."

Features of *The Inspiration Factor*

I get far more out of reading a book if I'm given an opportunity to take some time to wrestle with the issues the author presents. Perhaps you're the same way. For that reason, at the end of each chapter I have outlined on a week-by-week basis the outcome objectives you should strive to accomplish and a timeline in which to accomplish them.

To help you achieve those objectives, I've provided two lists of action items. The first, "Equipping Yourself," consists of thought-provoking questions that will give you valuable insights into your unique abilities to inspire people and will stimulate rich discussions. The second, "Inspiring Others," gives you concrete exercises to undertake to use those insights to inspire others. You can work through all of the action items or as many of them as time permits. Understand that the more questions you address and exercises you do, the better you will understand the inspiration process.

I recommend that you take advantage of "Going Deeper," which provides you and your team with a "challenge" assignment. This section is especially helpful in creating meaningful discussions in team meetings. No matter how you use this program, or how many of the objectives you have time to pursue, by following the guidelines in this book you will learn a lot about yourself and about how to help those around you—be they coworkers, family members, or friends, individuals, or groups—realize their full potential.

THE SEVEN PRINCIPLES

I've had the great privilege of rubbing shoulders with men and women who inspired me; now I want to inspire others. If you've picked up this book, it's fair to say that you, too, want to be someone who inspires and celebrates courage in other people's lives every day. That noble desire is one of the most challenging—and fulfilling—pursuits in life. How better to achieve life fulfillment than by inspiring another to greatness?

And here's the good news: though we come from different backgrounds with widely varied experiences, and our personalities differ in many ways, *every* person is uniquely equipped to inspire others.

Years ago, I began my career as an inspirational speaker addressing the toughest demographic group in America: teenagers. Three days each week on as many as three different campuses a day, I walked into auditoriums to inspire and motivate five hundred to five thousand teens. My goal was to help them find self-esteem in deeply held personal values rather than simply through performing on a competitive team or making good grades. I hoped to inspire them to make their decisions based on timeless wisdom instead of passing trends. It was during this time that I observed firsthand the truth in the saying "birds of a feather flock together."

Though the large-group presentations always seemed to go well, the breakout sessions were more difficult by far. Yet it was in those small groups that I learned how to inspire people even in the most hostile environments. Many times I had to face the cynical and critical attitudes of a group of students classified as "high risk." In the crucible of these demanding experiences, I began to see seven basic principles of effectively inspiring others that work in every market, culture, and demographic—even for high-risk people. They'll work for you too.

As you explore the principles, you will learn how to identify the embers in others, as well as how to fan those embers into flames of passion, loyalty, and excellence. These principles work in any context (with individuals, teams, divisions, or multinational corporations), so even if no one else in your organization "gets it," *you* can take the initiative and apply them—with outstanding results—to those under or over your leadership.

The seven principles are:

- Principle 1:   Be Authentic
- Principle 2:   Connect with Others' Dreams
- Principle 3:   See in Others the Abilities They Don't See in Themselves
- Principle 4:   Speak with Credibility
- Principle 5:   Tell Great Stories—Yours and Others'
- Principle 6:   Help People Reach Their Destination
- Principle 7:   Create a New Culture

Each of the remaining chapters focuses on one of the seven principles. If you commit to following these principles, you will discover the powerful results that the inspiration factor can have on your own life and the lives of others. What's more, with diligence, you can—and will—create a culture of inspiration in just twelve weeks' time.

My Promise to You

Many of you have attended management seminars until your derriere ached. Then you went back to your workplace, took a step or two to implement the techniques you learned—but little happened. What, you are probably asking, will be different about the information in this book? Great question.

The principles you'll probe in *The Inspiration Factor* focus more on character than technique. When we learn to be true to ourselves—to take off our masks and become authentic—then we will care enough about people to uncover their dreams and value their abilities. Thereafter, we'll develop ways to intrinsically motivate them. In a nutshell, we'll focus more on right priorities and less on the bottom line.

The principles in this book are designed to allow you to use the inspiration factor to raise the inspiration factor in the lives of others. Applying these principles takes some intention and effort, but they will have a multiplied, powerfully positive impact on you, on the people around you, and on everything you touch. And here's my promise to you: If you take the time to work through even one of the seven principles in this book and meet the objectives at the end of the chapter, it will move the needle forward in your ability to inspire others. Go through the entire twelve-week program, and you will change the very culture in which you live and work. Innovation will replace inactivity; sluggishness will transform into service. And the very atmosphere will change from one of self-interest into one bursting with cooperation. What could be better than that?

Before you read further, I recommend that you spend time in a short warm-up session. To reinforce in your mind our new definition of the word *inspiration*, ask yourself the following questions and practice the exercises provided. These Outcome Objectives and "Equipping Yourself" and "Inspiring Others" action items are representative of what you'll work through for each of the seven inspiration factor principles later in the book.

So, get going and get inspired!

GET INSPIRED—REDEFINING INSPIRATION

Outcome Objectives for Week One

- You will be able to talk about who and how key people in your life inspired you.
- You will be able to be specific about who is in your inner circle, that is, the people you want to inspire.
- You will be able to clearly identify what inspires each of your team members and your key customers/clients.
- You will be able to describe how your company/organization is making a difference in the world and how that can be inspiring.

Equipping Yourself

1. Reflect on what you draw inspiration from in your own life. Who is the one person who has inspired you the most? What specific things did he or she do to raise the inspiration factor in your life? What impact has this person made on you?

2. Make a list of eight to ten people who are in the center of your life today. Who inspires you the most on a *regular* basis, and why?

3. Draw a horizontal timeline on a piece of paper, beginning with your high school years and ending with today. Now record on this timeline each of the successful periods and discouraging periods you've experienced. Finally, place the names of inspirers and windspirers from your life chronologically along the timeline. As you look at the chart, what conclusions do you draw about the impact of these people on your life?

4. Think about your customers, clients, donors, and children. How would you rate your inspiration factor in these relationships on a scale of 0 (nonexistent) to 10 (off the charts)? Explain your answer.

Inspiring Others

1. Ask your team members what attracted them to their present position, and create an inspiration profile for each individual. What inspirational tools will drive them in the direction of their desired goals? How can you positively motivate them to perform at their best?

2. Talk individually with your team members about the people who are central to their lives today. How do these people inspire them?

3. Show your team members the timeline of the most successful periods and discouraging periods in your life and the names of those who inspired you and those who drained your inspiration. Talk about the impact these people had on your life. Encourage your team to think about one successful period and one discouraging period in their own lives. Who inspired them and who discouraged them? How did this happen?

4. Ask your team to think about their customers and clients. How would they rate their inspiration factor in these relationships on a scale of 0 (nonexistent) to 10 (off the charts)? As you discuss their answers with each team member, talk about the inspirational relationship you have with your own customers and clients.

GOING DEEPER

- How is your company (or nonprofit organization, church, or family) making a difference in people's lives?

- What are some real-life stories about how your company is making a difference?

- How is your team contributing to this effort? What is your team doing well? In what areas does your team need to improve?

- How is each individual contributing to this effort? In what aspects of work does each team member feel most fulfilled? Most frustrated?

Be Authentic

Authenticity means transparency, freedom from pretense. The ego is terrified of authenticity.
—Andrew Cohen, American author, artist, musician

PEOPLE CAN TELL. We might be able to fool them for a while, but sooner or later, they can always tell whether we're real or not, and their perception of our authenticity defines our relationships with them.

Whenever I teach our Raising Your Inspiration Factor seminars, I typically find a time for participants to share what they consider to be the defining moments in their lives. It's a powerful and effective way to get people to open up. Authenticity must include a level of transparency, a degree of vulnerability, and a heavy dose of genuineness. Sharing with a group your defining moment in life is a safe way to begin to practice authenticity.

In a recent seminar in Los Angeles, participants told stories of failed marriages, bankruptcy, illness, prodigal children, and other gut-wrenching difficulties. They opened the door to a room in their hearts (for some, that door had been closed for a long, long time), and the whole group connected with them. Each person shared how he or she had mustered the courage to take steps forward and find hope for the future. Each step brought new insights, and for many, the most painful moment in their lives ultimately proved to be a turning point toward more hope, love, and joy than they'd ever experienced.

As each participant talked, the rest of us felt their pain and marveled at their courage, knowing that it had required a great deal to turn calamity into better fortune. As each one returned to their seat, people reached out to offer a high five or a touch on the shoulder. It was wonderful. I specifically recall one CEO talking about how the previous year had been a defining moment for his business. He shared with the entire group how the economy had made things more challenging than ever and how he had lost a lot of sleep worrying about how he and his team were going to pull through. He went on to explain that during a company-wide town hall meeting, he laid it all on the line—the good, the bad, and the ugly. He concluded by saying how moved he was by how many of his associates stepped up and turned things around.

A few people at the seminar kept the door closed, however. They weren't willing to be vulnerable with us, and from their expressions, it appeared that they weren't willing to be honest with themselves. They knew they had to say something, but they settled for bland, superficial statements. One man, for example, talked about getting a speeding ticket, and the only lesson he learned was that he needed to get a radar detector.

In another case, a woman tried to talk about the strained relationship she had with her sister, but her explanation was so full of excuses and obfuscations that none of us could follow the trail of her thoughts—and we were convinced that she couldn't either. In the end, she hadn't learned any lessons at all because she hadn't been honest with herself about the pain she had experienced.

Another individual, who happened to be the supervisor of several other seminar attendees, told me he was especially perturbed at me for putting him on the spot by asking him to reveal his personal struggles in front of people he had to supervise. He was clearly bothered that his direct reports might see him as anything less than "professional" and "together." I explained that this exercise was meant to create a level of discomfort but not to embarrass anyone. I assured him that he was free to share or not share but if he chose to share, it would have the complete opposite effect of what he anticipated. Rather than think less of him, his team would actually think more of him for being transparent and vulnerable.

In contrast with the rapt attention given to those who were authentic, listeners shifted in their seats, looked down instead of at the speaker, and coughed at odd times when those who were emotionally disconnected spoke. Even after these speakers sat down, the room was filled with tension.

My experience at the seminar that day showed me more clearly than ever that those who are authentic about their pains and joys connect with people on an emotional level and have the greatest opportunity to inspire them. They have proven that even the most devastating problems in life don't have to crush us: they can make us stronger. Their stories of pain and courage break down walls of suspicion and build bridges of respect and trust. And their authenticity provides a safe haven for others, inviting them to uncover their own fears and dreams.

Another way to say all of that is simply this: don't waste your pain! Learn from it. Teach from it. Inspire others by being true to yourself about it.

So, What's *Your* Story?

People who have gone through life's gristmill and found hope on the other side don't flippantly say, "I turned my scars into stars," or "I changed my importunities into opportunities." (This kind of language makes me cringe.) Superficial platitudes diminish the pain, the agonizing process of growth, and the courage required to overcome difficulties. *Real*, hard-won triumph over indisputable adversity results in positive and *profound* stories, never superficial ones. And these should be told with authenticity and vulnerability.

Find one person at work that you trust, and take one step toward being authentic with him or her by opening a door in your life to an event that you would consider a defining moment. Begin there, and watch the inspiration factor rise.

It's All About Trust

In a 2007 *Washington Post* article titled "Three Words for the Next President," Pulitzer Prize–winning political columnist David Broder observed, "Authenticity means comfort in one's own skin, a minimum of pretense or artificiality, and especially consistency and predictability on matters of principle." When I go to a meeting, a convention, or even a dinner of hundreds of people, I can usually pick out those who are comfortable in their own skin. Actually, if you know what to look for, you can find them fairly easily. They are the ones who aren't trying to impress anybody. The look on their faces and their conversations tell you that they accept themselves for who they are. They know very well that they have flaws, but they also know their strengths, and they value them.

Because they accept themselves, they can look beyond themselves to genuinely care about *other* people. And they do. These people ask great questions, and they really listen when people respond. That's attractive in any setting! Further, when they speak, they do so without ostentation. They don't *need* to put on airs. They know who they are, and they have no problem being authentic about it.

Authentic people . . . don't try to impress anybody; accept themselves for who they are; know they have both flaws and strengths, and value them; genuinely care about other people; ask great questions and listen attentively; speak without ostentation; don't put on airs; and know who they are.

Authenticity is the foundation for building trust in any relationship—at work, at home, in the neighborhood, on the team, and everywhere else we go. Tragically, many of us spend an incredible amount of emotional energy and time trying to be someone we're not. We wear masks to project an impressive image or to hide a fragile psyche, much like the buttoned-up supervisor from Los Angeles I mentioned earlier. Funny thing is, he knows he doesn't have it all together, and his team certainly knows that too. They had just never let him know it. He assumed his mask was holding up to the task.

Wearing a mask, though, is surprisingly hard work. In fact, it's exhausting! It means being on the alert at all times, looking for the right people to impress and searching for the right thing to say to them. Our adrenaline level is sky-high because we're afraid we'll say or do the wrong thing. Then, when we do, we relive those actions and conversations, condemning ourselves for the dumb things we've said or done. That's not the way to live. As Peruvian author Carlos Castaneda once said: "We either make ourselves miserable, or we make ourselves strong. The amount of work is the same." Why not work toward being authentic?

Now, all of us want to make a good first impression and try to present ourselves in a positive light. That's not what I'm talking about. I'm talking about *wearing a mask*. Why do we do it? Because, I think, at the core of our lives lies fear. I should know. I wore a mask myself for a long time. We put on a psychological mask when we feel insecure and want to make up for it. We may project enormous confidence, but behind the facade, we are afraid of being exposed as failures, ostracized by those whose opinions we value, or, in a word, *rejected*.

So, the mask goes on, and with it we try to convince others that we're smart, witty, cool, or classy. These masks really aren't much different from the ones we wore as children for Halloween. They accomplish the same exact things, too: changing the world's perception of us while hiding who we *really* are. And worse, many of us have worn a mask for so long that we have no idea what it's like to be authentic and to live without one.

Our words, clothes, cars, gestures, hobbies—everything about us—are all designed to win approval, gain acceptance, and even to *control*. Why? Because, regrettably, in some organizations masks are valued more highly than authenticity, and those who project a particular image get the job and the promotions. So, on goes the mask, and we think it's working, but in reality, we're driving people away, because they sense that we don't care enough about them to be authentic. In a phrase, they can see right through us—and that's anything but inspiring.

Who comes to mind as you think about people you know who wear masks? Are they good leaders? Do they inspire you? I doubt it. But they're everywhere to be found, and they try to fool almost everybody around them. Have you ever noticed that everywhere you go, you meet the same people; it's just the faces that are different when it comes to masks. Some of the more popular masks I have encountered are these.

- The Reaper. This is the individual who thrives on the reputation of "going after heads." Reapers manage by intimidation and feel it necessary to terminate someone from time to time to serve as an example for the team. I actually met this person on the job some time ago. She had seven pennies on her file cabinet and was not real discreet about who those pennies represented—one for each person she was committed to terminating. Each time one of these persons was released, she would have a penny-dropping ceremony in her office. Again, I know these things solely because she made it known to others around her. There is a lot of negative motivation going on around this mask wearer, but I assure you, there is no inspiration.

- The Parent. This is a popular mask because it makes the person wearing it feel needed and significant. As you can tell from the name, this person's role is to protect and preserve those he likes. The parent language is quite noticeable: "You need to . . ."; "That won't work—we tried that a long time ago." Some employees take comfort in having someone tell them what to do. But for those who are looking to be inspired, being led by a Parent mask wearer is a bad fit.

- Captain America. Careful not to reveal any real emotions, this mask wearer effectively projects complete dignity and utter competence. As with any mask, though, it does not allow others on the team to relate or connect to its wearer. Always right. Always confident. Never inspiring.

- The Multi-masker. You never know exactly which mask this individual may be wearing from one day to the next. Depending on the situation and the circumstances, he or she can change with a moment's notice. The culture the multi-masker desires to create with this mask is one of fear and paranoia, keeping the team off balance and on edge.

I opened this chapter, if you remember, with the simple declaration "People can tell." Masks can, in fact, effectively fool others—for a short time—but inevitably, if we keep those masks tenaciously plastered to our skins, people realize they aren't getting the real thing from us. Then the problem isn't just the mask; it's the cold, calculated fabrication behind it. People will no longer trust us. They won't accept our attempts to motivate and inspire them. And they certainly won't let us into their lives, because we haven't let them into ours.

To be authentic, though, doesn't mean that we have to expose all the refuse of our lives for others to see. Yes, we must let others in if we hope to inspire them, but we must also be discerning when determining how much to share, when to share it, and with whom we share it. Just as people distrust those who wear masks, they likewise distrust those who delight in describing—in great detail and with great frequency—their pain and frustration. This often comes across as just an attempt to get others to feel sorry for the one who is sharing. That's hardly a recipe for inspiration.

We must let others in if we hope to inspire them, but we must also be discerning when determining how much to share, when to share it, and with whom we share it.

But when people are straightforward and authentic as they share their difficult experiences, making sure to top off their stories of hardship with the crowning ingredient—the *lessons learned*—they become heroes who can genuinely inspire others. Putting a positive spin on a negative experience turns a depressing part of your life into an inspiring one. If you do this while reflecting on all the difficult parts of your life, you will find redemption and peace instead of bitterness and longing.

I'm reminded of a young woman I met who was in an abusive relationship in high school. We'll call her Nicole.

The young man Nicole loved had beaten and intimidated her to the point that she had lost all confidence in herself. After a while, she deferred to him in every decision, even what and when she ate. She was emotionally crushed, only a shell of the vibrant young woman her family and friends had known.

On the day of her graduation, Nicole told her parents and siblings that she was pregnant. Aware of her boyfriend's abusive treatment of Nicole, they insisted that she never see him again. She was too emotionally dependent on him, however, to break off their affair. But after several months of her parents' pleading, she finally came to a point of decision. Her parents had talked to friends across the country who were willing to let Nicole live with them and raise her baby in their home. They had found a job for her too. The choice was excruciating for everyone involved, but Nicole promised she would go.

Just hours before the flight was to leave, she was about to back out. Finally, a good friend offered to go along, and together they got on the plane and headed west.

Over the next six months, Nicole hung on to the possibility of being reunited with her boyfriend. She heard rumors that he had a new girlfriend and that she, too, was pregnant. But old dreams die hard, and Nicole still hoped he would take her back. As time passed, though, hope turned into despair.

When the baby came, Nicole poured herself into her daughter. Gradually, her depression faded, and faint glimmers of hope began to reappear: not hope for reconciliation with her boyfriend but hope for the *future*—hers and her child's. She worked and went to school to earn a degree. She developed a new set of friends, people who loved her but didn't try to control her. And as the years went by, she grew stronger and more resilient, with more hope for the future than she ever dreamed possible.

Today, her wisdom and love make her a magnet for other women in abusive relationships, and she helps them out of the wealth of her experience. Her story is a tragic one with a glorious ending, and she tells it authentically but also with discretion. In so doing, Nicole *inspires* everyone who knows her.

It would have been much easier for Nicole to hide behind a mask. She could have chosen to live in shame and silence, keeping her story to herself. But authenticity pays great rewards. Perhaps the greatest reward will come in the future, when her daughter is grown and can genuinely grasp the immensity of her mother's bravery. The sad story of a girl who made a bad relationship decision will also be a story of a mother's undaunted courage to face reality, make hard choices, and carve out a new, hopeful, productive life for herself and her child. Already, this young lady inspires people, but because she took off her mask, her impact will only grow as time goes on.

What about you? Have you taken off your mask, or are you still wearing one? "What do you mean?" you might ask. Well, for example, have you ever been in a place of leadership but felt totally inadequate? It is at precisely those times that you may be tempted to wear a mask—to project strength that isn't there, to protect yourself from exposure, and to keep your feelings—maybe even your inadequacies—hidden. You may feel incompetent, threatened, and vulnerable, but believe it or not, these can become your finest moments of inspiration. This is when you need to muster the courage to remove your mask and honestly say to those who look to you, "*I need you*." That's authenticity: admitting that you need your team and that you can't make it through this time without them.

Now, watch their response. The vast majority of people react very positively to such authenticity. It's the seed of trust that can grow and blossom into strong, effective relationships. It's also the seed of inspiration. Working for a man or a woman who is unafraid to admit to occasional fear and weakness will cause others to be able to admit the same. Soon *everyone's* masks come off, and it is at this point that teams can really begin to work together, their guards down and their cooperation up. That's the inspiration factor at work.

In order to be the most effective that you can be at inspiring others, it pays to know what type of leader you are.

Know Yourself, Be Yourself: Four Inspiring Personality Types

Many of us labor under the misconception that we have to have a Tony Robbins personality in order to inspire people, but that's simply not the case. God has made *all* of us with a unique blend of personality, talents, gifts, and strengths, and with them, we can inspire others. And the more we discover and live by our own God-given attributes, the more fulfilled, effective, and inspirational we'll be.

For centuries, philosophers have recognized four distinct personality types, or "humours," as they were once called. The ancient Greeks believed these emanated from four bodily fluids. Recent (and decidedly more scientific) research has also recognized four distinct personality types. Books such as Florence Littauer's *Personality Plus* and *The Four Elements of Success* by Laurie Beth Jones discuss these in detail. Another great source of information about personality types is the Personality Dimensions website and its self-discovery system (www.personalitydimensions.com). For our purposes, I have identified four inspiring personalities: the Commander, the Coach, the Advocate, and the Accountability Partner. Your personality and the personalities of the people you lead are a combination of these four types. Let's examine them one by one.

THE COMMANDER

For the most part, my clients are academic health care centers. Among them, many colorful and powerful personalities converge as they seek to uncover what I believe will be the greatest discovery of our generation—the cure for cancer. Because of my involvement with this industry, I get to witness the blending—and clashing—of all four of the personality types I've labeled. I also get to see their various approaches to the issues they're facing.

Some people face every day with the mentality of a warrior/fighter. My client and friend Dr. Donald Trump at the Roswell Park Cancer Center in Buffalo, New York, is one such individual. His every waking hour is consumed with keeping alive the vision to find a cure for this dreadful disease while he goes head-to-head with congressional bureaucrats for more funding. At the same time, he manages to earn the loyalty of a heavily recruited research team, meet with patients and their hurting families, and so much more.

Dr. Trump is the consummate Commander. His personality type equips him to assimilate huge amounts of data as he makes life-altering, high-impact kinds of decisions.

Commanders inspire others by their boldness, confidence, and determination to succeed. They are motivated by challenges—the bigger the better—and they marshal every resource to accomplish their lofty goals. They cast a bold vision, and they make decisions quickly. Above all, they value action, not just words and emotions. Examples of Commanders include some of history's great military leaders, such as General George Patton and Napoleon. If you are a little short on your history, we can point to people in our own time, such as management expert Jack Welch or, better yet, the fictional character Miranda—played by Meryl Streep—in the 2006 box office hit *The Devil Wears Prada*.

At their best, Commanders accomplish incredible feats by marshaling resources and challenging people to excel. At their worst, they try to control people by intimidating them. Unfortunately, under stress, such bold and determined Commanders become so fixed on their goals they can forget that people have feelings. They can be impatient and demanding, determined to press ahead at any cost. Threats become their primary motivational tool, and they lose the respect of those closest to them. I've known Commanders who inspired their people by their clear, forward vision and their example of humility and brilliance, but I've also known men and women who, when the chips were down and their organization's future was on the line, yelled, cursed, and blamed everybody else for any perceived failure.

If you are a Commander, you are probably an outstanding leader when things are going well: you excel at communicating vision, organizing people, and setting an example of courageous, effective action. In times of stress, though, you run the risk of using instead of leading people to get what you demand from them. What you need to remember, even in the good times, is that other personality types on your team may need more affirmation than you normally give, or more explanations of the reasons behind your decisions. To inspire them, slow down a little, ask a few questions, and value their responses. Let the team come up with suggestions instead of bulling ahead with your own decisions.

THE COACH

I recently had the opportunity to attend a team meeting led by one of my favorite colleagues at Grizzard Communications Group. I can't even recall what the meeting was about, but what I do remember is her leaning over the table, looking into the eyes of the thirty or so people present, and working them as a tent evangelist. So inspiring was my colleague that she probably could have asked this group to accept a pay cut and they would have done it—and felt good about it. That's because my colleague is a Coach.

Coaches are personable, enthusiastic, and persuasive people who thrive on using their personality/persuasion to influence others. Their greatest strength is their ability to notice what people do well, sincerely affirm them, and put them in a position to succeed. In fact, when everyone on the team is succeeding, Coaches are at their best. They care about their team members, so they are most fulfilled when everyone is encouraged—especially when the people above and below them show appreciation for their efforts. Some examples of prominent Coach-types are Herb Kelleher, former CEO of Southwest Airlines, and comedian/activist Bill Cosby.

On the negative side, Coaches sometimes become enamored with the sound of their own voices and consequently talk too much. And under stress, they may lose focus; their thinking can become disjointed. In fact, Coaches can be surprisingly fragile and feel easily hurt. When this happens, they can become defiant and demand that others take sides—for them or against them. I've known athletic coaches, corporate executives, and other leaders who loved to build people into a cohesive unit to fulfill a high purpose. That's what Coaches do. But I've also known a few who, under pressure, lost their way, became distant, and blamed others for their own mistakes.

If you are a Coach, people love to be on your team because they know you genuinely care about them as individuals and will do anything to help them excel. But remember that some people will be frustrated if you talk too much without giving clear direction and letting them take action. Other members of your team need to be able to ask questions and get real answers, not just your "happy talk."

During times of stress, avoid labeling people as pro (all for you) or con (all against you), and avoid the extremes of blind optimism and bleak despair. In difficult times, ask questions—and *listen* to the responses. Value the varied contributions of each individual on the team. In place of just a "pep talk," provide clear direction for everyone, and give individual attention to questions from others.

THE ADVOCATE

When I first joined Grizzard Communications Group, I had the privilege of working under Advocate Claude Grizzard. Claude was easy to like: He was always willing to yield to better ideas, and he was absolutely fabulous at engaging people in problem solving. As chairman of the board, he certainly had both the knowledge and the authority to say and do whatever he thought was best, but he thrived on involving *others* in the process.

I remember one day when Claude got a group of us together to discuss an issue that had surfaced the day before. He actually started the meeting by saying, "I misspoke yesterday on this matter, and I just wanted to clear the air." Claude is obviously very sensitive to the feelings of others. This is typical of Advocate-types.

Advocates are also creative and reflective. They value loyalty in relationships, so they make a few really close friendships. They are inspired by opportunities to be thoughtful and original in planning. And they ask a lot of questions, not because they want to challenge authority but because they sincerely want to know the whys of every decision. Trust and the freedom to be imaginative are two premier values for Advocates.

Advocates thrive on new ideas and creative approaches—things that drive some of the other personality types crazy. Furthermore, they inspire *others* to contribute their innovative ideas for problem solving. The best teachers are probably Advocates who patiently instruct and inspire their students.

In the business world, Advocates form strong relationships and often see potential that others have missed in people. I've seen Advocates have a profoundly positive impact on people who felt lost or overlooked by others. Their sensitivity, though, has a dark side.

Advocates can crater under pressure, becoming discouraged and indecisive. Then, confused and seemingly lost, they revert to their analytical world instead of staying engaged in solving the problem. Even in the good times, they need a lot of individualized attention. But under stress, they need even more, when less is usually provided. And though change is the very lifeblood of other personality types, Advocates typically view change as a threat—especially during times of stress—and need plenty of time to respond to it.

If you are an Advocate, people trust you because you are loyal, sincere, and patient with them. You naturally nurture others, but you do not provide much challenge. And remember that some individuals thrive on risk and action, the opposite of your profile. Although others appreciate your thoroughness, they don't necessarily want to go too deep into the relationship. Learn to value their devotion to precision, but don't expect much of an emotional connection with them. Finally, a few folks just want clear direction in order for them to make their optimism and energy effective. Make sure to give it to them.

In stressful times, Advocate, *be careful*. You can easily be run over, because you tend to become negative, overly sensitive, and hesitant to make decisions until you have all the answers. Drum up the courage to step back into the fray and move forward, even if you feel somewhat uncomfortable with the level of risk.

THE ACCOUNTABILITY PARTNER

Not long ago as I was working with a particular organization, I noticed a pervasive skepticism throughout the rank and file of the company. Most companies I talk to are very energized at the prospect of creating a more inspiring environment. Not so with this company. Every idea was met with a "we've heard that before" kind of response. That's because team members had heard plenty of optimistic prattle and lofty propositions, but there was never any follow-through. Why? Because the team had no Accountability Partner.

Accountability Partners are critical to a team and are inspired by opportunities to concentrate on and follow *prescribed* systems to obtain *measurable* results. They lead best in organizations that value precision and tight controls. Because they are so detailed and disciplined, they consistently turn in excellent work even on the most mundane assignments; they especially thrive in stress-free environments where expectations are clear and deadlines are firm.

Accountability Partners can become top executives in highly analytical or technology-related companies, but they play important roles in any organization. Their discipline and thoroughness give them the ability to help people do what they've already committed to do by asking questions and checking schedules. In other words, they inspire others to be more *disciplined* in order to be more *effective*.

Under stress, though, Accountability Partners tend to isolate themselves—especially from angry or out-of-control people—and revert to systems they can control. They feel very uncomfortable with risk and change of any kind. Their commitment is to the *details*, and their hyper-attentiveness to the fine points can make them appear harsh and judgmental, especially when they feel pressure to make others toe the line.

If you are an Accountability Partner, people value you because you are so devoted to excellence, but they may not understand what makes you tick. In good times, your clarity of expectations gives everybody a smooth track to run on. Be sure, though, to value the entrepreneurial spirit of your teammates. They don't care as much about systems as you do, but they are willing to take risks that keep the organization moving. Advocates value reflection and detail, as you do, but they care more about feelings. Inquire about their personal lives, and then listen.

In times of unusual difficulties, when you are tempted to hide from people and find security in the systems you know so well, remember that people need you. Get out there, interact with them, ask questions, affirm them for trying to find answers, and give them pats on the back for each step toward success. You have the ability to help people stay focused even in the middle of chaos, but to play that role, you have to stay engaged and not retreat.

One example of an Accountability Partner is Jim Donald, former CEO of Starbucks. He was initially hired because of his expertise on efficiency: the customer was standing in line too long for his drink. Operations were so efficient under Donald's leadership that the coffee experience itself seemed to become secondary, and Howard Schultz, who demonstrates a lot of Coach-like attributes, was asked by the board to come back as CEO.

Warning!

A word of warning: Far too often, we value only the Commanders and the Coaches as inspiring personalities because they are the most verbal and visible. What's worse, these strong personality types often pigeonhole the Advocates and Accountability Partners as "too analytical" or "too negative"; meanwhile, they themselves are often the most inauthentic people in the organization, ensuring their failure at inspiring *anyone*. My experience shows, however, that *every* person can play a valuable role in inspiring others—*whatever* their personality type. Begin by discovering who you are, and be true to yourself.

Some of us have a clearly identifiable personality type, but most of us are a combination of two or more of the four types. Take some time—right now—to go online (www.inspirationblvd.com) or to appendix A in this book, and take the Inspiration Blvd. Personality Profile to identify your personality type. Your scores will show you whether your profile consists of one or more than one type. As you analyze your scores, keep in mind such factors as your stress responses and where you are in the organizational hierarchy. Many of us respond differently under stress from the way we do normally, and some of us relate up the ladder in a very different way from the way we relate to peers or those who report to us, so keep these things in mind.

Understanding your personality type will allow you to learn your strengths and weaknesses, to be comfortable in your own skin—and therefore to be *authentic*.

To make this principle real, I often ask seminar attendees to complete the Inspiration Blvd. Personality Profile, and then I organize the entire room by the four personality types, one type in each quadrant of the room. Then I simulate a problem and ask each personality group to talk among themselves and determine how they would go about addressing the problem.

As each group proposes its solution to the simulated problem, it's both comical and enlightening. Every Commander knows with all confidence what needs to be done and who needs to be enlisted to get it done. The Coaches are convinced that if people would just get passionate and focused about it, the problem would take care of itself. The Advocates feel certain that any solution will first require the formation of several committees to consider the matter, offer input, and reach a consensus. And of course, the Accountability Partners want to know "What does success look like?" and "What are the steps and resources needed to get there?"

What workshop participants learn through this activity is that every personality is important. In addition, because it becomes clear that one type is not any more significant than another, people feel safe to remove whatever masks they had been wearing before and be who they really are.

Authenticity requires both a dose of knowledge and a measure of courage. Taking an inventory of your personality traits will give you some insight, but it's up to you to have the courage to yank off your mask and lead authentically. But if you will do it, people will trust you, and you will have taken the first step toward *inspiring* others.

GET INSPIRED—BE AUTHENTIC

Outcome Objectives for Weeks Two and Three

- You will be able to list the values, benefits, and risks of being authentic.
- You will be able to identify which personality type(s) fit you best, and why.
- You will be able to identify a primary attribute of each personality type and how each type is wired for being inspired—and for inspiring others.

Equipping Yourself

1. Without writing down any names, identify someone who wears a clearly identifiable mask. How would you describe this mask? What image does its wearer project? What might he or she be trying to hide or protect?

2. What are some ways that mask wearing prevents authenticity? What is the effect on the person wearing the mask? What is the effect on that person's relationships with others?

3. Pinpoint a time or an occasion when you yourself put on a mask. Was it during a presentation? At a company party? While visiting your relatives? How did wearing a mask affect the way you related to others?

4. Complete the Inspiration Blvd. Personality Profile, found either online or in appendix A. Does one of the four inspiring personality types seem to fit you, or are you a combination of personality types? When you go into a problem-solving mode, what personality type do you most easily relate to?

Inspiring Others

1. In a discussion with an individual on your team, ask the person to identify someone he or she knows outside of work who wears a clearly identifiable mask: perhaps an uncle who is always the life of the party, or a coworker who always uses self-deprecating humor. Then ask: "How would you describe this mask? What image does its wearer project? What might he or she be trying to hide or protect?"

2. Ask your team member the following: "What are some ways that mask wearing prevents authenticity? What is the effect on the person wearing the mask? What is the effect on his or her relationships with others?"

3. Ask the individual to pinpoint a time or an occasion when he himself was the mask wearer. Was it during a presentation? At a company party? While visiting with relatives? How did wearing a mask affect the way he related to others?

4. Share with the person the results of your personality test, and your analysis of it. Then ask the person to take the personality test, analyze it, and discuss the results with you. What actions can each of you take to inspire one another and the others on your team?

5. Discuss with the individual how understanding your personality type has made you become more authentic. Then ask him, "How do you think understanding your personality type could help you?"

GOING DEEPER

Ask your team to:

• Explain how accurate (or inaccurate) they believe the Inspiration Blvd. Personality Profile is for them.

• Discuss the specifics of what motivates them on the job and what kills their inspiration.

• Share the insights they've learned about each other after they've heard other team members explain their profiles.

Connect with Others' Dreams

*Run your fingers through my soul. For once, just once, feel exactly what I feel,
believe what I believe, perceive as I perceive. Look, experience, examine,
and for once, just once, understand.*
—Anonymous

I WANT TO BEGIN this chapter about connecting with others'
dreams by sharing a story. It's about a young man—we'll call him Rick—
who graduated from a prestigious university with a degree in marketing.
Soon thereafter, he landed a job with an ad agency in Denver.

> For the first few months, Rick described his position as "a dream come
> true" because he got to work on national accounts with his colleagues, and
> he felt he was making a significant contribution. As Rick became more
> comfortable in his role creating ad campaigns and designing the ads, the
> owner of the company praised him to employees and clients alike. Never-
> theless, at every meeting and in every way, the owner himself found a way
> to become the center of attention. Rick accepted this behavior as normal
> for someone who had taken the risk to start a company.

A few months into Rick's employment, a crucial deadline for the company's major client approached, and the owner's demeanor changed drastically. He was no longer the lighthearted, creative leader Rick knew him to be. He turned into a bear. In meetings with the creative team, the owner blurted out idea after idea without asking for or accepting input from the rest of the team. Rick tried to offer his opinion a couple of times, but the owner blew him off and chastised him for being "so negative."

The atmosphere of the entire company changed during those intense weeks. Everyone tiptoed around the owner in fear of getting chewed out, and seldom did anybody offer an opinion on anything. It was like a big, awkward dance, with every person moving in tandem with the owner's mood. Creative people, though, can't stand it when they aren't allowed to express their ideas, so several team members tried again and again to offer suggestions. (They knew better than to tell the boss that his ideas were bogus.) Still, the owner didn't listen to anyone about anything. The whole world, it seemed, revolved around "the boss."

One day, a woman who had joined the company a year earlier than Rick had offered a creative concept in a meeting, but once again the owner ignored her. After the meeting, she wrote down her idea and put it on his desk. A few days later, he bounded into the conference room to announce his "bold, new, innovative idea." It was hers, but he didn't give her any credit at all. He claimed it was his brainstorm.

This experience taught Rick that the company's actual mission was very clear and very limited: to make the owner a hero at all costs. After the first few thrilling weeks on the job, Rick gradually realized that his contributions would never be valued, and he dared not ever express his dreams. They wouldn't matter to his boss at all.

Notice, Name, and Nurture

We all have dreams and desires. They may be big or little, outward or inward, clear or cloudy, but unless we are severely wounded emotionally and are hiding in a shell of self-protection, we all have aspirations. One of the most significant insights of my life is that I, as a manager, can tap into my employees' dreams and reap rich benefits for them, for me, and for the company.

After all, any company's overall success can be highly compatible with each person's cherished desires—enough so that everyone feels fulfilled. Of course, not every person's dream is for the company to succeed, but most—especially those whose own needs are being met—*will* achieve personal satisfaction from the company's success. Why? I believe that God has put it in the hearts of all people to live for something *bigger than themselves*.

At the same time, however, most folks enter their profession with the hope that their career within a successful company will help them achieve *their own* life's dreams as well. One of the greatest joys of my life, therefore, is uncovering others' dreams and providing resources to fulfill them. I'm sure you feel the same. To do that, you need to *notice, name*, and *nurture* their dreams.

NOTICE DREAMS

We *notice* others' dreams when we watch their faces and listen to their voices to see what thrills or impassions them. Some of our dreams are self-focused: to own a second home in the mountains; to tour Europe every year; or to have enough money for a comfortable retirement. Another layer of our dreams, though, connects our skills with our hearts. We may want to be a motivational public speaker and shape others' lives; we may want to lead a group of people who want to grow richer and stronger in some way. But many times, our dreams are shaped by a need we feel called to meet. We may want to pour our resources into supporting an orphanage, building low-cost homes, or caring for the elderly.

If we ask a few questions, we can often quickly discover what makes people tick. I ask questions such as these:

- "What attracted you to the company?"
- "What activities energize you and feed your soul?"
- "What keeps you up at night, either from worry or excitement?"

- "Where do you think you can have the greatest impact?"
- "Do you feel more comfortable with relationships, facts and figures, or managing processes effectively?"
- "If you could write a slogan for your life, what would it be?"
- "What makes you cry, and what makes you laugh?"

Many employees think that the only thing their managers care about is their performance and their contribution to the bottom line. Sadly, they're often right. But if we ask questions such as these, we will uncover real dreams—and a person's dreams are the source of his inspiration.

NAME DREAMS

As I've talked to hundreds of men and women over the years about their dreams, I've discovered that putting a *name* to these dreams makes an enormous difference. I listen intently as they answer my questions, and then I might say something like the following examples to summarize their responses:

- "You never give up. You're a true *competitor*. What's your favorite kind of competition? How are you presently using that competitive spirit in your day-to-day activities? Have you considered how that competitive nature could be aligned with your career? Is there something you've always dreamed of doing that would allow you to take full advantage of this God-given competitive nature?"
- "You have an intuitive ability to sense what people are thinking and feeling. You also have a high degree of empathy, a good heart, and a lot of emotional intelligence. Do you presently find your ability to be empathetic useful in your day-to-day work? If so, how? There's a lot of opportunity for people with your ability. What kind of things have you dreamed about doing that would take full advantage of that gift?"
- "You are so persuasive—but without being pushy. I've never seen a better promoter. Where did you learn to persuade other people like

that? Did you ever have any career aspirations that would require you to use the art of persuasion?"

- "You have an uncanny ability to assimilate an enormous amount of information, yet you are also really good at connecting the dots to create a clear picture of what's really going on. That's a very good leadership trait. I'm curious; what kind of goals do you have that would allow you to really use that ability?"

Observing people's strengths should lead you to uncover and name their dreams. Quite often, the act of naming their dreams crystallizes people's thoughts and gives them a handle on the future they've never had before. Your involvement is a tremendous gift to them. You may be the first person ever (or at least in a long time) to have investigated, uncovered, and invested in their dreams.

Quite often, the act of naming their dreams crystallizes people's thoughts and gives them a handle on the future they've never had before.

Let me give you an example from my own career that illustrates this beautifully.

Several years ago, I was looking for someone to help with creating proposals. One young lady in particular had a very intriguing background. Her résumé showed some great experience in creating sales proposals, but it wasn't altogether different from many others I looked at—except that it revealed that she had also tried her hand as an off-Broadway actress. It was not very difficult to uncover her dream to be an actress. Still, I took time to notice and acknowledge it.

During the interview, I was truly curious about how her experience brought her to this point and how I might uncover her dream, tap into her strengths, and align her personal passions with what we needed on our team. As I probed about the off-Broadway experience, I asked, "What was it that you loved about that experience?"

"It was all the things that led up to the performance that were energizing to me," she answered. "The building of the props, working super-late nights with other performers, and the pressure to get it all together on time and in excellent form."

I immediately said, "You have the job." My promise to her was that she would be able to use this work environment as a way of continuing to hone those very skills for wherever they may take her in the future. And in the meantime, I had a very specific business objective, and I needed her best stuff to accomplish it.

Now, I think she would have taken the job anyway. But being able to name her true dream and align it with our business objective made for a compensation package that went far beyond money. That's the inspiration factor at work.

NURTURE DREAMS

Noticing and naming are important, but the third ingredient—nurturing—is crucial too. When people have trusted us enough to share their dreams, we need to *nurture* both them and their dreams. One of the best ways to do so is to provide resources and advice so those dreams can be fulfilled. In the vast majority of cases, people were attracted to their current roles because they consciously or unconsciously saw their jobs as channels of opportunity to fulfill their dreams. For that reason, it's usually not difficult to help people see how their daily responsibilities could be stepping-stones to those goals.

In some cases, a major reassessment of a person's job description may be required, but it's worth it, because aligning an employee's personal dreams with the company's goals makes for a powerful combination. It unleashes amazing energy and creativity in that individual. On the other hand, when personal goals and company goals *cannot* be aligned, every activity seems to be forced.

How do you even begin to align an employee's dreams with corporate objectives? Considering the person's best interests is a good starting point. Leaders should make every effort to see to it that what's *best for the employee* is a high priority, even in the midst of pursuing the company's goals. This commitment from leaders optimizes employee performance, reaps outstanding results, and smoothes any necessary transitions. If you are a leader, look aggressively for opportunities to develop, train, and expose your people to others who can help them reach their dreams. That's nurture.

For the past twenty years, I've followed this process of noticing, naming, and nurturing the dreams of people who report to me, and almost without fail, it has changed the atmosphere of the office. When people are convinced that we genuinely care about the deepest desires of their hearts, they become more enthusiastic, creative, disciplined, committed, and flexible than ever before. I know. I've seen it over and over again. But when we fail to connect with their dreams, the air turns cloudy (if not poisonous), energy evaporates, and suspicions multiply. People feel used instead of valued, and they are easily distracted by anything and everything.

Leaders should make every effort to see to it that what's *best for the employee* is a high priority, even in the midst of pursuing the company's goals. This commitment . . . optimizes employee performance [and] reaps outstanding results.

Why Don't We Connect?

The diagnosis is easy, but the treatment is difficult. The primary reason we, as managers, parents, and other leaders, don't connect with people is stress. We don't pay attention to the desires, needs, and dreams of others because we're too hurried and harried—that is, too "stressed"—to think about anyone else.

Actually, stress isn't the problem; *excessive* stress is. In his book *Margin: Restoring Emotional, Physical, Financial, and Time Reserves to Overloaded Lives*, physician Richard Swenson observes that moderate levels of stress bring out the best in people. Appropriate challenges stimulate creativity and inspire people to accomplish higher goals. As with the proverbial "frog in the kettle," however, our stress levels can increase so gradually that we don't even notice.

The danger, of course, is that excessive levels of stress can begin to feel normal; we're lulled to sleep, and worse, in that bath of boiling water. Although we experience the detrimental effects of too much pressure, we fail to take note of the underlying problem, and correspondingly, fail to make changes. Under intense pressure, every aspect of our lives is affected: our abilities aren't as sharp, we make bad decisions, patience evaporates. Consequently, we experience even more stress.

In many cases, we even experience physiological symptoms, such as headaches and stomach problems; our most important relationships suffer; and we become less and less effective, which eventually leads us to feel discouraged, depressed, and burned out. In other words, our focus soon becomes *our* health, *our* emotions, and so on. It should come as no surprise, then, that the greater the stress, the higher the self-preoccupation—and the lower the inspiration factor.

There is probably little that causes more stress these days for a corporate leader than striving to make Wall Street happy. Much of the time, those things that drive market value up and down are out of the control of the CEO. I have had the fortunate experience of seeing our own CEO at Grizzard Communications Group pass the stress test with flying colors. He's a true competitor in both his personal life and in the way he does business. He refuses to allow market pressure or internal pressure to steal his personal sense of well-being. The outcome of his ability to not let the pressure beat him is the high-producing group of leaders around him, whose average tenure is more than ten years.

At the other end of the spectrum, I observed another CEO insulate himself from the very people who could and would have helped. He believed that the only way to manage his way out of trouble was to unilaterally cut costs. Without driving the inspiration factor up, you will never be able to cut enough costs to reach a sustainable level of success.

The pace of life today is far faster than it was in earlier generations. We demand quick solutions instead of expecting change to take place over several seasons and to involve long processes. We have redefined "normal" as swift, complete resolution to life's problems, and we are annoyed with anything less. With our RAZRs, BlackBerrys, and iPhones in hand, we expect to get more done in less time, and we rush from one thing to another, trying to turn a busy life into a full life. Amazingly, though technology has promised to give us more free time, we actually live at a more frantic pace, with less time for reflection, leisure, and relationships. It's no wonder we're stressed.

Today, people I call "hurry-sick" leaders are in a world of their own. But to inspire other people to greatness, these men and women have to get beyond their own world and reach into the worlds their staff inhabit, connecting with their dreams. Leaders *can't* connect with them, though, while rushing past them to get more stuff done. Such leaders have to change their values, to define the difference between what is urgent and what is not so important and focus on the *truly* important things in life—the people around them.

A friend of mine told me about a pediatrician who had cared for his little girl years ago. The pediatrician was an eminent doctor who served on several boards and at one time had been the president of the American Pediatric Association. Few professions are more demanding than being a doctor, and this man's schedule was packed beyond belief. Nevertheless, when this doctor walked into the examining room, "He acted like there was no other child in all of God's creation—only mine," said my friend. He continued: "He gave my daughter complete, focused attention, and he patiently answered every question we had. And in fact, he took time to give my wife a recipe for dressing at Thanksgiving. I don't know if I've ever felt as cared for in all my life."

When we make people a priority, we take time to notice more than the obvious traits that everyone sees. For example, I used to introduce my team members at presentations by listing their titles and accomplishments, but as I've become more observant, I now introduce them by describing the impact of their talents and identifying their aspirations. I'm not so sure that customers or clients really have any sense of what our industry-oriented titles really mean, anyway.

So, rather than introducing Christy McWilliams as our account director, I say, "I'd like to introduce you to the person who is going to make sure you get the results that we promise." We have an incredibly talented creative director, but I don't think my clients really know what that title means, so instead I introduce him this way: "Please meet Douglas Broward. He is the one committed to making sure your creative presentation is on brand, relative, and effective."

The real fun in this started when I began having each of our team members introduce the others. It was amazing what they "noticed" and "named" about their colleagues.

This subtle shift changes everything. My team members feel understood and valued, and our clients realize that we practice what we preach about making people a priority. It raises the inspiration factor for every person in the room.

> I now introduce my team members by describing the impact of their talents and identifying their aspirations. The result is that they feel understood and valued, and our clients realize that we practice what we preach about making people a priority.

In that light, I want to introduce you to Scott Thompson, someone, I believe, who does an outstanding job of taking time to notice the dreams and strengths of the folks on his team. Scott is the vice president of development for the University of Arizona Cancer Center in Tucson. Going to see Scott is always a learning experience for me. Most of my clients are quick to "look at the numbers" and see how we are doing relative to projections. Scott is the only client I have who spends the first forty-five minutes talking about *every one* of his direct reports. He always sees the best in them. He is constantly making organizational adjustments to maximize his team's talents. What's impressive, above all else, is how he could tell you—to the person—what his team members really wanted to be when they grew up.

Most people in his role have a top-ten list of individual and corporate prospective donors. I am confident that Scott does too. But his priority is the building and nurturing of his team. He takes time to inspire because he knows the outcome will be good for the university, the contributors they serve, his team, and himself.

Each of the seven principles in this book offers us a choice: to keep going the way we've been going, with the same, predictable results, or to change. As long as we let stress rob us of our time, drain our energies, and erode our passions, we'll continue to miss golden opportunities to notice, name, and nurture others' dreams. If, however, we intentionally carve out space in our lives to live for the things that are truly important instead of being harassed by the urgent, we'll have plenty to give to others. Change requires insight, commitment, and courage; insight comes first, and we gain insight into people only by taking time to notice, name, and nurture their dreams. Is it worth it? You have to decide for yourself. From my experience, I think it is. My wife, children, interns, employees, and friends would say so too.

Connecting with the Dreaded "Performance Review"

Many of us, managers and employees alike, dread annual performance reviews because we perceive them as disruptive, negative, or shallow. Let me offer a different approach: Ask your team members to identify at least three personal dreams and connect those with corporate goals. The performance review can then focus on clarifying the person's dreams and the specific ways the company can become a vehicle to help that employee fulfill her greatest desires. Your role will be to provide training and other resources so that the company's objectives become a platform for the employee's passion, skills, and energy. You can imagine the enthusiasm this discussion will generate!

This past year, for instance, I asked one of our team leaders, "What are you dreaming about these days in terms of your future? Is there something I can support you in that would make you a more valuable employee while helping you toward a personal goal?" She became animated and talked about her desire to get her MBA but was uncertain about how to fit it into the rest of her priorities. As I assured her of my support and willingness to allow for a more flexible schedule, she could not have been more enthusiastic. Taking the initiative, then, to write that as a goal on her performance review for next year solidified her confidence in my commitment to support her.

Bear in mind, this was not an offer to pay for her extended education, but a promise to be supportive and flexible with her work schedule so she could do what was in her heart to do. Did I win a measure of loyalty from her? You bet I did. And as a company, we are going to have a more valuable employee.

CONNECT OTHERS' DREAMS TO PERFORMANCE REVIEWS

Tom Harrison is the chairman and CEO of Diversified Agency Services (DAS), which manages Omnicom Group's holdings in a variety of marketing disciplines serving national and international clients through more than 700 offices in 71 countries. Tom is an innovative leader whose passion is to inspire an entrepreneurial spirit in his team and with his clients. To make sure the executive leadership of the 160 DAS companies feel challenged and inspired, he hosts three biannual gatherings, called Jazz Meetings, so the leadership can come together, hear a great speaker, discuss an important topic, and learn creative ways to serve their employees and clients more effectively. He also launched a blog to help the Omnicom family tap into the entrepreneurial DNA of its clients.

As every top manager knows, there's an inherent risk in stirring up innovative, aggressive team members: some of them may start competing companies. But this possibility doesn't bother Tom. He believes that an environment that encourages creativity and risk taking will attract and retain outstanding men and women. And he's right. Executives at Omnicom are convinced that Tom cares passionately about them, their individual dreams, and their shared dreams because he's tapped into precisely what they're good at: entrepreneurialism. Instead of holding tightly to their reins, he's actually encouraging the very entrepreneurial spirit that could one day make them "the competition"—and they know it. But rather than wanting to leave, his execs want to stay. Under Tom's umbrella, they are fulfilling their dreams.

You may not be at the top of the corporate ladder as Tom is, but you can still connect with others' dreams, even at the lowest management level. Let me offer a few specific suggestions to help you use annual performance review sessions to identify people's dreams and to provide the right resources to fulfill them.

Help people craft a personal vision statement.

Notice that I didn't say, "Tell them to write a vision statement." Far too frequently, when people are told to write a "vision statement," they come up with something that isn't compelling and fails to capture their hearts. Crafting a personal vision statement is a process that shouldn't be rushed. For it to be effective as a life marker, it has to reflect the person's genuine desires, ones that may be hidden behind her own masks and the expectations of others. The questions designed to uncover a person's dreams are a good place to start (see pp. 41–42), but don't stop coaching people until they have crafted something that makes their eyes light up and their hearts sing. It's work, but it's worth it—for both of you.

One of the best resources to consult when writing a personal vision statement is *The Path: Creating Your Mission Statement for Work and for Life* by Laurie Beth Jones. She instructs people to begin by listing words that describe their abilities and character, not just their titles or roles. For some, this exercise is a struggle at first, but soon they realize that they are far more than salespersons, administrators, managers, or consultants. They are, instead, *caring, dedicated, loyal, trustworthy, helpful, kind,* or *visionary.* As these words are used to craft a personal vision, a powerful new sense of direction begins to unfold. (Go to inspirationblvd.com for an exhaustive list of descriptive words that can jump-start people's visions of and for themselves.)

Create an environment where it's safe to take risks . . . and fail.
Some people, like Commanders and Coaches, love risks. They thrive on competition and challenges—the bigger the better. Most folks, however, see risks as threats instead of opportunities. Our job is to help them face their fears and overcome them so that risks actually become opportunities for growth.

Here's an anecdote involving my oldest daughter that aptly illustrates my point.

> When Brittany began to play tennis, she was afraid of hitting the ball out of bounds or into the net. Like the vast majority of beginners, she tentatively hit the ball in a soft loop to maximize the possibility that it would stay within the court. I knew that with this approach it would take her a long time to develop the skills and confidence she needed to excel at the game.
>
> "Brittany, don't worry about hitting the ball out of bounds or into the net," I told her. "You can hit it out, or you can hit it into the net, just don't hit it like a sissy. Hit it hard!"
>
> She hit it hard. In fact, she smoked the ball on every shot! Soon she began to learn how to control her stroke, so more and more shots were good. Before long, teammates, coaches, and parents were amazed that she hit the ball so powerfully and accurately. Now she hits the ball harder than anyone I've ever played. But she could never have done it had she continued to allow her fear of making mistakes dominate her game. To succeed, she first needed permission to fail. And when I gave it, Brittany experienced freedom to learn and grow.

The same principle works in business. Let's say you have an employee who is unaccustomed to contributing in a meeting because it is not her personality or she assumes it is too risky. What do you do?

We were recently faced with just such a situation. A relatively quiet young woman joined our team from the client side of our business. One day, to my surprise, another team member shared with me that this young woman has an MBA and is serving in a much lesser role than she is qualified for. After the next team meeting, where she was once again relatively quiet, I invited her to stay and chat for a moment.

"I'd be very interested," I began, "in learning some things that you, as a former client, know about us, and how we could do better. And if possible, I'd like you to lead us in that discussion next week." She was a little taken aback but was more than willing to step up. She was incredibly well prepared at the next meeting, and her insights were hugely valuable to us. It was exactly what needed to happen to bring her out. She has since demonstrated initiative on multiple projects.

Mark Twain said: "Twenty years from now you will be more disappointed by the things you didn't do than by the ones you did do. So throw off the bowlines. Sail away from the safe harbor. Catch the trade winds in your sails. Explore. Dream. Discover." Many people fail to pursue their dreams because they feel caught in a web of fears—the fear of failure, rejection, being exposed, looking silly, and others. When we give such people a safe place in which to take risks, free of condemnation for failure, they respond like a bullet shot from a gun. They take off! Some, though, aren't sure we really mean it. They're afraid we'll criticize them or correct them (or even terminate them) if they fail. Reflective, suspicious people need more time to be convinced that we mean what we say, and often, they need to see us give others freedom to fail before they themselves will take risks.

> Many people fail to pursue their dreams for fear of failure, rejection, being exposed, looking silly . . . When we give such people a safe place in which to take risks, without being condemned for failure, . . . they take off!

A few people have an inherently negative attitude about their jobs. To them, work is supposed to be boring, demanding, and difficult. Failure, they believe, is an institutional and personal norm, and the concept of aligning their personal dreams with the company's objectives isn't even on their radar. These people need a radical reorientation about the meaning of work. For them (and for everyone on your team) I suggest that you take time at an upcoming team meeting to stake out a new direction.

First, write your company's goals on a whiteboard or poster and explain: "This is where the company is going. Any questions?" Then give each person a piece of paper and ask them to describe the kind of reputation they want among other employees, management, and clients or customers. Give the group a few minutes to complete this task. Then ask them to write a list of the specific activities they can perform that will both achieve the corporate goals and enhance their reputations. After they've written their responses, provide plenty of time for people to share their answers, and sincerely encourage them to share their insights.

Don't stop there, however. Tell them you want to meet with each of them individually to fine-tune their plans. Then, in the weeks that follow, meet with each team member to affirm him, adjust his job description if necessary, and set new expectations. This process can reenergize every person in your office and foster a willingness to step out and attempt bold ventures without fear of censure.

Provide regular, specific affirmations.

Many managers and parents make one of two common mistakes (or maybe both): (1) They make the colossally inaccurate assumption that if people are doing well, they don't need affirmation; or (2) When they do affirm, they use global, nonspecific language. Neither inspires anyone. And know this: Whether your job is managing or parenting, *everyone* around you is thirsty for affirmation. In fact, some of those who seem to want it least actually need it most. A wise person once said, "People live for encouragement, and they die without it." Every person, even those who seem to be rock-solid islands of stability, needs others to notice and celebrate what they do well.

Sandy is a young lady who works for a nonprofit organization, and everybody marvels at her skills and temperament. One day, her CEO told me, "Sandy's an exemplary employee. If I could craft someone using someone else's DNA, that person would be just like Sandy. She is bright, kind, creative, punctual, and a great team player."

"Have you told her that?" I asked him.

"At her last review," he replied.

"When was that?"

"Six months ago."

I pressed a little. "I'm quite sure she'd like to hear you say that she's a valuable person on your team. You may not know it, but some other companies have heavily recruited her. She chooses to stay because she is committed to the mission here."

He thought for a moment and then said, "No. I don't think she cares what I think about her. She's strong. She doesn't need that kind of coddling."

Sandy's CEO is dead wrong. Dreams die for lack of nurture. On the other hand, regular, specific affirmations are the sunlight, water, and fertilizer of people's dreams. To be meaningful, though, they have to be specific. Telling someone, "You're great!" doesn't mean very much at work, at home, or in volunteer organizations. Study the people who report to you, and verbalize the positive things you see in each one. (If each person takes the Inspiration Blvd. Personality Profile, you'll have a lot of specific information to work with.)

When we fail to affirm people, we unwittingly create an environment where suspicion and distractions grow. People want to know where they stand with their manager. When they hear nothing at all, or hear only corrective words, doubts and insecurity begin to form. In this atmosphere, people become easily distracted from the task at hand, preoccupied, instead, with self-protection. They start spending time imagining what might be going on behind closed doors or thinking about finding another job. Teams, like all relationships, don't remain static: they are continually in the process of growing stronger or weaker, of building or eroding trust. To keep the whole team strong, *every team member* needs to be affirmed.

When employees receive management's affirmation, the company's mission becomes the employee's mission. There is a direct correlation between affirmation and loyalty. In fact, show me a leader who is slow to affirm, and I'll show you a group of employees with wandering eyes and hearts.

Observe people's positive emotional responses.

Some of us are astute in noticing the negative responses we see in others, but we need to be just as aware of their positive responses. Obviously, when we see someone's eyes light up with excitement, it is evidence of a desire being fulfilled (or at least addressed). But enthusiasm isn't the only positive response to watch for. When people are gripped with the dream of making a difference, they are passionate about those they want to help. Passion may surface as joyful exuberance; it may also appear as a "holy disgust." Many leaders observe that real change often comes only when people become truly disgusted with the status quo. Something, these fed-up souls determine, simply *has to* change. Their attitudes are similar to that of Popeye, who when reaching the tipping point of exasperation, growls: "That's all I can stand. I can't stands no more!"

When you see enthusiasm in someone, don't take it for granted. Explore it, ask questions, and pursue the underlying motivations. And when you see holy disgust, don't be alarmed. Anger at injustice and tears of compassion are good and right. In fact, they are obligatory for a healthy person with a dream to make a difference.

Be a resource to help people reach their dreams.

Your words of specific affirmation are vital, but words aren't enough. Your commitment to people—and your ability to truly inspire them—is demonstrated when you take *action* to help them progress toward their dreams.

It's really not that hard. Let me give you two illustrations from my experience.

A young man on my team once told me that his dream was to learn to be a public speaker. So, one day at lunch we went to the bookstore and I bought him a CD of great speeches. He was blown away. A few minutes and a few dollars convinced him that I was going to be his number one fan, and our relationship rose to a new level that day. Another time, I was on the receiving end of just such affirmative action. I mentioned to my good friend Laurie Beth Jones over lunch one day my keen interest in studying the great speeches of the twentieth century because I wanted to be a more effective communicator. The next week she sent me a beautiful book containing fifty of the greatest speeches of the last one hundred years. I appreciated her kindness even more than the book itself.

Valuable resources are readily at hand. HR departments can help managers identify courses, seminars, coaching, degree programs, and countless other opportunities to help employees reach for their highest goals. Too often, though, these resources remain underutilized simply because managers fail to ask about them.

Celebrate every step forward.
Great managers make a big deal out of people's progress, and they are creative in their celebrations. They know that recognizing achievements doesn't have to be expensive to be meaningful. You can throw a party at the finest restaurant, or you can call your team together and give them a certificate of appreciation to commemorate their accomplishments.

And achievements worth celebrating don't have to be limited to those that happen in the company. You can just as easily memorialize a person's accomplishments *outside* the office walls. I've heard of one district manager of a large company who even appointed one of his team members as the unofficial director of ambience. This person's job is to keep celebrations and affirmations high on the priority list and make sure they are meaningful.

You should do the same. Remember, people are trying to reach their dreams. Each step toward those dreams is one step less they have to take to fulfill them. Celebrate!

The Risk of Dilution and the Power of Alignment

Over the years, as I've talked to executives about these principles, most of them intuitively grasp how they can inspire their people more effectively. Yet for a few, the attitude seems to be: "Who's got time for all this inspiration stuff? We've got jobs to do and results to produce." True, inspiration does take time, and so does connecting with other people's dreams. And *too much* focus on individuals' dreams can dilute a team's energy and take attention away from the corporate vision.

But I've seldom seen this problem occur. More often, I've seen corporate and nonprofit executives wringing their hands because their people are negative and critical. They've tried myriad techniques, carrots, and sticks, but little has changed.

Yet, when we tap into people's dreams and show them how the corporate vision can be a vehicle to help them reach their goals, we experience the incredible power of alignment. It's a beautiful thing to see, and often it happens almost spontaneously. Time after time as I've watched people uncover their dreams, they've become more committed to the company than ever. More than that, their trust grows in the manager who cared enough to talk to them about what matters most to them. I've seen good employees become great, and those who had been labeled "problematic" become effective, pleasant members of the team.

Is it important for managers to learn to align the company vision with each person's dreams? Yes. In fact, I believe it has a multiplied impact. The ability (or inability) of managers to inspire their people shows up in tangible ways, such as higher or lower profits, and in intangible ways, like the way employees connect with customers because they feel affirmed and supported. And as I've alluded to earlier, it makes a difference in employee retention. People send résumés to a company because of the company's brand and reputation, but they usually leave because they can't stand their supervisor. Employees deeply appreciate supervisors who genuinely care about their dreams and support their efforts to reach them.

For years now, I've started team meetings by asking people to share what positive traits they've noticed in each other. At first, people talked about task-related things they'd seen: "Penny, you stayed late to finish that report," or "Your presentation was excellent, John. You were really well prepared." These comments were very encouraging, but in a month or two, people began to notice and name character qualities, not just performance: "Susan, you showed a lot of courage when you handled that client," or "I couldn't believe how patient you were, Phil, when that guy kept asking the same questions!"

As people felt more understood and affirmed, they were more open to sharing their dreams with the rest of us. Gradually, everyone realized that we valued more than each person's performance; we valued one another. As I reflect on a particular team that gelled especially well, I realize that we had at least one of each of the four personality types in our group, and they noticed different abilities and strengths in each other.

Valuing people beyond their performance is important in families too. Robert Lewis, in *Authentic Manhood: Winning at Work and Home* (both the DVD and the workbook), observes that there are three statements every child needs to hear often: "I love you"; "I'm proud of you"; and "You're good at [a skill, talent, or activity]." These statements, when spoken from the heart, give a child (or a spouse, for that matter) a strong foundation for pursuing his dreams for the future. In the inspiring words of Henry David Thoreau, "I have learned that if one advances confidently in the direction of his dreams, and endeavors to live the life he has imagined, he will meet with a success unexpected in common hours."

The same is true in the marketplace. Inspired employees make life much more enjoyable for their managers. Team members accomplish more, so Commanders are happy. Team members work together more effectively, so Coaches feel fulfilled. When employees feel free to try new things and make mistakes without being condemned, they become more creative under the leadership of Advocates. And inspired employees aren't as resistant to following rules and using systems, so Accountability Partners can sleep well at night. When employees' dreams are noticed, named, and nurtured, everybody wins. Start doing it today. It's a choice that only you can make.

GET INSPIRED—CONNECT WITH OTHERS' DREAMS

Outcome Objectives for Week Four

- You will be able to know how to uncover the dreams of your team members and align them with corporate goals.

- You will be able to help your team members write a personal vision statement for their lives.

Equipping Yourself

1. Ask yourself the following questions. Answer them honestly, and make note of your observations.

   - "What attracted me to the company?"

   - "What activities energize me and feed my soul either at work or outside of work?"

   - "What keeps me up at night, either from worry or excitement?"

   - "What events, relationships, needs, and challenges of the past year have generated the most passion in me?" (Explain what happened and how you responded.)

   - "How would I describe how I want my life to count? What kind of impact do I want to have?"

   - "If I could write a slogan for my life, what would it be?"

   - "What are some resources the company and I can provide to help me have that kind of impact?"

2. When you've finished asking yourself these questions, complete this sentence: "From what I've just said, it seems that my life's dream is to . . ."

Inspiring Others

1. Select someone on your team with whom to practice the notice, name, and nurture principle. Who comes to mind? Take time to record your perceptions, as well as the outcome of your inspirational transactions, in a journal. Remember to

note the strengths that you noticed and not so much what the person did but the character trait you saw him or her demonstrate through action.

Share your observation with that particular team member. What can you do to nurture what you observed?

2. Set up an uninterrupted time to talk with each person on your team about his or her dreams. Prepare for each interview by writing down at least two specific strengths you see in the person and, if possible, identifying the topics that have evoked positive emotions.

Begin by explaining that you want to get to know each person on the team more fully, and you want to ask some questions about what matters most to them. Explain to the interviewees that you have asked yourself these questions, as well, and tell them about your own dreams.

As you ask these questions, listen intently, and ask follow-up questions. If the person says something significant, you can say, "Tell me more about that." You might ask, "What happened next?" or "How did that affect you?" Don't rush through the questions. It's better to have a rich discussion about one or two of the questions rather than to try to cover all of them. The questions are:

- "What attracted you to the company?"
- "What activities energize you and feed your soul either at work or outside of work?"
- "What keeps you up at night, either from worry or excitement?"
- "What events, relationships, needs, and challenges of the past year have generated the most passion in you? Explain what happened and how you responded."
- "How would you describe how you want your life to count? What kind of impact do you want to have?"
- "If you could write a slogan for your life, what would it be?"
- "What are some resources the company and I can provide to help you have that kind of impact?"

When you've finished asking the questions, or feel you've asked enough of them to have had a valuable discussion, summarize by repeating what you heard the person say. Make this statement in terms of the person's dreams: "From what you've said, it seems that your life's dream is to . . ."

Then ask, "What are some ways I can help you take steps toward your dream?" Listen carefully. People may not believe you really want to help, or they may not have any clue about steps they need to take, so they certainly can't explain how you can help. Don't push this offer, but tell the person that you'll be looking for ways to help in the future. Thank him or her for the time, and end the interview.

3. Within a few days of the interview, take the initiative to mention the person's dream again, but not in a public, potentially embarrassing way. You might ask people to share their dreams in a team meeting if they feel comfortable talking about them. Mutual understanding and support can work wonders to build trust and cooperation!

GOING DEEPER

- At least on a monthly basis, talk to each employee about his or her dreams, and ask what you can do to help. Find resources and look for alignment within the company so that the company's goals become stepping-stones for the person's growth.

- At a team (or family) meeting, ask, "What difference would it make if each of us individually and all of us as a team aligned our dreams and abilities with the company's (or family's) goals?"

See in Others the Abilities They Don't See in Themselves

Finding the right work is like discovering your own soul in the world.
—Thomas Moore, Irish poet, singer, songwriter

A PERSON'S DREAMS and abilities are inextricably linked, but they aren't the same thing. One is about the heart; the other is about the hands. Dreams tap into people's deepest desires and strongest motivations, but they can wither and die if they aren't nurtured. We must help the people we lead maximize their strong suits—their talents and innate abilities. Only then will they feel enthused about what they do every day.

When I was just in the eighth grade, I already had a glimmer of a vision for my future. I wanted my life to make a difference, and I believed that my future would involve communicating verbally and in writing. At the end of that year, my English teacher announced to the class, "If any of you would like to take a creative writing class, let me know." I jumped at the chance. I raised my hand and told him that I wanted to sign up.

He frowned and said: "I don't think that's a good idea for you, Terry. You struggle too much with your writing now. There's *no way* you can make it in that class." Needless to say, I was hurt and disappointed, but I determined even then to not let someone else's weak opinion of me hold me back.

In stark contrast, that same year my history teacher saw more potential in me than I saw in myself. I was only a mediocre student to that point, and though he and I hit it off well in class, I didn't make stellar grades in history (or any other class, for that matter). At the end of the first term, he sat at his desk, looking at the honor roll list. After a few minutes, he looked up and said: "Mr. Barber, I don't see your name on the honor roll. I certainly thought you'd be on it."

"Me?" I replied incredulously. Nobody had ever told me he expected me to be an honor student.

"Of course," he replied with calm assurance. "You're bright, you grasp concepts very well, you're curious, and you have what it takes to be a very fine student." He smiled and nodded toward me. "I expect to see your name on the list in the future."

Until that day, I had made Bs and Cs in all my courses, but from that moment on, I never made anything less than an A in history.

The Power in Recognizing Potential

One of my favorite client contacts is incredibly competent when it comes to all things CRM (customer relations management). But as she herself confessed, when her company decided to acquire a new CRM system, Heather was fearful she would not be intuitive enough to "get it," much less help lead the charge to communicate to the rest of the team that this was really a good change.

Prior to the big announcement to the group as a whole, her supervisor met one-on-one with her. "Heather," she said, "I realize you are probably just as concerned about having a smooth transition and grasping a whole new system as your teammates are, but I really need you to help create a positive and receptive climate. I am confident of your ability to learn this system—you're a quick study, and you have great skills. But more important, your character will enable you to be a strong leader for this endeavor."

Whatever fear Heather had about the new system was instantly minimized by a word of confidence from her boss, who saw in her what she did not see in herself. The bottom line in this situation? Heather "got it," made it look easy to her teammates, and in no time, everyone in her department was proficient in the new system.

POTENTIAL VS. PERFORMANCE

There are plenty of B- and C-grade types in the workplace who need someone to see the potential in them and ask them to accept a challenge. But let me be clear: I am not suggesting that you promote people just because you see potential in them. I didn't earn an A just because my history teacher found potential in me. I did the work he inspired me to do. Similarly, Heather didn't "magically" learn the new system just because of her boss's encouragement. She spent hours studying and practicing before she presented the new system to her team.

We can be inspired by management's recognition of our potential. We will certainly be motivated by any further recognition of our potential. But in business, if we are to be promoted, we are required to *perform* at an A level.

The Power to Build or Destroy

As managers, leaders, teachers, and parents, we have the amazing power to build or destroy, to be a launching pad for success or to crush people under the weight of discouragement. Our ability to recognize others' abilities makes an enormous difference in their motivation, their confidence, and the course of their lives.

THE POWER OF SPEAKING WORDS OF ENCOURAGEMENT

Overcoming ingrained negative messages is a lifelong chore; it requires persistence, courage, and the support of at least one person who believes in us. Some people never make it. But I'll give you an example of one who overcame, and by doing so she became one of the most prominent figures in our culture.

We know her as the queen of daytime television. She is so popular that she is recognized instantly by one name: Oprah. Her face is familiar to people around the world, and she is an icon of strength and hope for the hurting, the disillusioned, and the abused. Few people, though, know the real story of Oprah's rise to fame, wealth, and influence.

She was born on a Mississippi farm to a maid and a soldier. When the couple separated just after Oprah's birth, the infant was left in the care of her maternal grandmother, Hattie Mae Lee. This loving woman had great dreams for the abandoned little girl and refused to see her as hopeless. Instead, she inspired Oprah to aim for bigger things—much bigger things—than her dismal situation suggested she could achieve. Because of her abandonment, Oprah could have grown up feeling like little more than a throwaway. But Hattie Mae's constant encouragement was the little girl's bedrock of confidence upon which she stood and reached for the stars.

When she was six, Oprah moved to Milwaukee to live with her mother. There, a teenage cousin, other male relatives, and their friends molested her. She could have given up, given in to depression, exploded in rage, or turned to a life of promiscuity, but her grandmother's voice echoed in her heart: she *could* be somebody special.

Finally, when she was thirteen, she ran away from home and moved to Nashville to live with her father. Oprah's father valued education, and he immediately began to put her through a rigorous program. For example, he wouldn't let her sit down for dinner each evening until she had learned five new vocabulary words. His prodding and high expectations met their match in the ambitious teen, and she thrived. Still, it was her grandmother's direction that paved the way for her success. Recalls

Oprah: "My grandmother really raised me to be who I am because of her belief in education. Even though she wasn't very educated, never finished high school, she was strong."

The first public acknowledgment of Oprah's abilities came in the form of a $1,000 scholarship for a speech she gave in high school. Soon, other accolades followed. She became the first black woman to win Nashville's Miss Fire Prevention title, and she was Miss Black Tennessee.

Oprah landed her first job at a radio station in Nashville when she was seventeen, and two years later, a television station hired her as a news anchor. She graduated from Tennessee State University with a degree in speech communications and theater, and soon thereafter she moved to Baltimore to not only continue her work anchoring the news but also to host a morning talk show, *People Are Talking*. She excelled in the interviews and exchanges with guests, and after eight years, a major station in Chicago asked her to host a talk show that was soon picked up by the network. The rest, as they say, is history.

The list of Oprah's awards and accomplishments would fill several pages. In the past few years, she has poured her influence and funds into efforts to improve the lives of desperately poor African children. Her daily TV show touches millions of lives each day, and her impact is truly global. Furthermore, Harvard Business School found her business acumen so impressive that on February 20, 2006, it published Martha Lagace's article "Oprah: A Case Study Comes Alive" in its *Working Knowledge* faculty research weekly newsletter (available at hbswk.hbs.edu/item/5214.html). None of this, though, would have been possible if a poor, uneducated grandmother had given up on a discarded child. Instead, she saw potential, and she inflamed the little girl's dreams.

In people's darkest moments they need someone to step into their lives, recognize their strengths and abilities, and give them hope for the future. For Oprah Winfrey, it was Hattie Mae Lee. She encouraged her granddaughter during the child's formative years to prepare for a bright future by pursuing education, inspiring her with the message: "No matter *what* you've experienced, you can still become someone special. *Don't ever quit.*"

Focus on the Positive

Many studies show that our self-perception is shaped to a significant degree in childhood by the messages communicated to us. In her article "The Positive-Negative Ratio," psychologist and author Sarah Radcliffe asks parents these practical questions: "Do you offer a steady stream of compliments, praise, and unconditional positive regard? Or is it, 'Hurry up! You're going to be late! Put that down before you break it! Clean up that mess right now! Eat your breakfast. Brush your teeth. Make your bed. The bus is coming. Leave your brother alone. Where's your homework?'"

Radcliffe recommends that parents give at least four positive messages (words, hugs, etc.) for every corrective one. For many of us, however, the negative messages we heard as we were growing up far exceeded the positive. It wasn't that our parents didn't love us; they just didn't know how to communicate it.

Even when the number of positive and negative messages is equal (or weighted toward the positive), sensitive people dwell on the negative ones they've heard. These messages cut like a knife, leaving the recipient bleeding and wounded. As adults, these people may receive many affirmations for their performance, but their minds remain haunted by statements such as:

- "You'll never amount to anything."
- "You're stupid."
- "Why can't you do anything right?"
- "I can't believe you messed it up again!"
- "You're a failure, and you'll always be a failure."

Today's effective managers are made up of a diverse set of ingredients: one part teacher, one part accountant, one part mediator, and two parts encourager. An HR director recently said to me after one of our seminars in Atlanta, "My work environment has become like an extension of high school these days." We had a big laugh about how analogous indeed it was. The outcome of our discussion, however, was just how much more important it was to be an encourager than ever before. Although it is not the job of any manager to "fix" an employee or to take on their emotional baggage, the fact is that a manager can move mountains in the life of an employee through the power of encouragement. This begins with a willful focus on the positive aspects of a person.

What do you focus on in your communication with employees, interns, team members, spouses, and children? When a child comes home with three As, two Bs, and a D, what do you react to and talk about? Most likely the D! Certainly, some corrective action needs to be taken in response to the low performance there, but the impact of focusing on the negative is devastating. The child would be far more encouraged and motivated if the parent celebrated the three As first before addressing the D.

Parents need to observe their children carefully to see how God has crafted them, with their unique blend of personality, gifts, and passions. King Solomon, one of the wisest leaders in history, wrote, "Train a child in the way he should go, and when he is old he will not turn from it" (Proverbs 22:6 NIV). Each child has a "way he should go" based on his character/ skill set blend. In fact, even children in the same family often differ markedly from one another.

To illustrate: I know a couple with three children. Two of them are very gifted athletes—the boy in football and baseball, the girl in volleyball. Both received college scholarships because of their superb athleticism. The third child, another boy, is about as coordinated on the field or court as cooked spaghetti. Yet early on, the parents—also very athletic— recognized that he had an innate musical ability. To their credit, they recognized and accepted the fact that he was different. They didn't criticize him for his lack of coordination; rather, they praised his ability to play the piano. They poured as many hours and resources into his musical development as they did into the lives of their kids who loved sports, inspiring their young artiste to musical greatness. In some families a child who is different is often ridiculed and labeled a "loser," but in this one, they all celebrate each other's successes. More power to 'em!

Positive messages can have a phenomenal impact. My wife, Debbi, remembers a specific conversation she had with her grandfather that inspired her for life. When she was eleven years old, she sat with him on a woodpile outside his home near Rome, Georgia. He was whittling. As they were talking, he suddenly stopped and turned his gaze toward her. "Debbi," he said, looking her right in the eye, "you're going to make something of yourself. I know it!"

At that moment, his words meant the world to Debbi, and to this day she still remembers his exact words and the look in his eyes. From that day forward, she has been strengthened by her grandfather's confidence in her. As she puts it: "If Granddaddy thought I could be somebody, who was I to argue with him? Even today, when I give a presentation, his affirmation continues to inspire me and give me confidence." Because this grandfather recognized a little girl's strengths, even when she could not, she was inspired to realize her potential.

When we go over an employee's performance review, do we breeze through the eighteen positive parts because "she already knows that anyway" and spend 90 percent of the interview on the two areas that need improvement? That seems a bit out of balance.

Marcus Buckingham, coauthor of *Now, Discover Your Strengths* and author of *The One Thing You Need to Know*, cites a study by the prestigious Purnell School in Pottersville, New Jersey, which surveyed employees' perceptions. From 2005 to 2007, the respondents were asked to record how much of each day they spent using their strengths. Over these three years, the answers slipped from a dismal 17 percent to 14 percent, and finally, to a tragic 12 percent. If managers want to motivate their team members by having them work in the areas of their greatest abilities and effectiveness, they clearly need to do a much better job.

In a talk he delivered at the Willow Creek Summit in August 2007, Buckingham identified several common myths about managing people. One of these is "You grow the most in the areas of greatest weakness." Not true, says Buckingham. Actually, people grow most in the areas where they are most confident and motivated: in other words, their strengths. When we focus our attention on their weaknesses, we stunt their growth and limit their potential.

I have a client on the West Coast who now heads up all major gift efforts for one of the most prestigious cancer centers in the world. She has personally been responsible for raising more than $150 *million* over the last ten years. Now, no one in the life of an academic institution is exempt from the political land mines. But in her case, the mines were more than political; they became really quite personal. Rather than noticing and nurturing this employee for all she has achieved, her boss consistently criticizes her for what he perceives as a weakness: her being a "working woman" versus staying at home to take care of her husband. I think it's fair to say this man has limited his best fund-raiser's potential.

When you focus attention on your employees' weaknesses, you stunt their growth and limit their potential. But when you, as a team leader, know the strengths of each person on your team and tailor assignments accordingly, they will contribute greatly to the team by exercising those strengths the majority of the time.

Here's another myth: "A great team member puts his strength aside and does whatever it takes for the team to succeed." This sentiment sounds noble and is occasionally true, but if it becomes the norm, the team member's motivation declines, and the whole team suffers. A person who contributes most to his team exercises his strengths the majority of the time. Team leaders, then, need to know the strengths of each person on the team—even if the member doesn't know them himself—and tailor assignments accordingly to fit as much as possible. The employees, in turn, will excel to a great extent by default. They're doing what they're good at, and when it earns them kudos, it will inspire them to do better still. And the gift goes on. Each new success will raise your team's inspiration factor by degrees.

A "360 Profile"

Before we can focus on others' strengths, we may need to begin with an analysis of how much we operate out of our *own* strengths. A number of self-tests and consultant-processed profiles are available to help people reflect on activities that have brought them success and fulfillment. Some of these go back to childhood; others center on more recent work experience. All of these, however, attempt to reveal patterns of experiences in the past on which to build a plan for the future. A successful analysis will uncover your primary areas of competence, interest, and fulfillment, and these should be reviewed in light of your personality profile.

One of the most helpful types of inventories is a "360 Profile" that provides insight from many different sources. Here's how it worked for me.

A set of questions about me was sent to my CEO, several peers, a couple of clients, my wife and children, and two friends. The feedback I received was fascinating, and in a few cases, very surprising. I was affirmed for my leadership and communication skills, but several people reported that I, like most men, sometimes fail to communicate as fully as I need to. In tension-filled situations, for example, I become very reflective and quiet as I carefully consider the alternatives and the consequences of those various choices. Some people were confused when I became quiet, however, because they expected me to be outgoing and verbal all of the time. The solution has been fairly simple. Now when I become pensive, I make sure to tell people that I'm not withdrawing from them and I'm not upset with them. I just need a little time to think. This single insight and adjustment has reduced confusion and raised the level of understanding. That's a very productive outcome.

The 360 Profile offers you the opportunity to solicit input from multiple sources—up, down, and across the organizational hierarchy, as well as outside it. If the questions are worded correctly, this tool promises to give you the most accurate feedback on your strengths and the areas in which you need to change or improve. A sample 360 Profile is included for your use in appendix B.

Opening Our Eyes

Why do so many leaders and managers fail to help others succeed? The answer, many times, is because they make false assumptions. Let me illustrate.

With regard to budgeting, many companies and nonprofits use what is known as "institutional budgeting" in which they assume that, since a given year's budget was just fine, they need make only minor adjustments to the following year's budget to see the same results. Unfortunately, many times we take this same approach with people. We make the assumption that they are doing just fine, but we're looking at them through the lenses of our *own* desires, needs, and goals. If they fit what we expect, we leave them alone to roll along again for another year . . . or another decade. Before long, we find that we are, to borrow an analogy from *Good to Great* by Jim Collins, riding along with the wrong passengers on the bus, or with people in the wrong seats, because we haven't taken the time and trouble to find the best fit for them.

In contrast, I recommend a "zero-based budgeting" approach to analyzing the strengths and weaknesses of your team. Start from the ground up each year as you think through goals, objectives, and budgetary allocations. This approach takes nothing for granted. It looks at the cold, hard facts, and opens eyes to greater opportunities. It shuns the status quo and concentrates on possibilities. It takes more effort, but it promises to be far more effective than the institutional budgeting approach to working with people.

When we put a team together, we should begin with no assumptions. We can then take time to ask questions, uncover dreams, identify abilities, and help people become great. If we become leaders of an existing team, we may have a bit more work to do, because the culture has already been established to some degree. Still, a little time, a few great questions, and good listening will bring to the surface the dreams of each team member. Then we can make adjustments to their roles so they can be more motivated and effective.

The same principles and processes apply if we are already leading a team. We can carve out time to dig deeper into each team member's life to find out what makes him or her tick. We need to value the team as people—not as cogs in the corporate machine—and align their abilities with the company's goals so that we can inspire them to excellence.

As you learn more about each team member's personality profile, you can tailor your affirmations and challenges for each one.

- A Commander on the team won't care much about warm words, but he will almost burst with excitement when you look at him and say: "Jim, we have a really tough job to do, and I believe you're just the guy to get it done. Are you up for it?"

- An Advocate might wilt if you took that approach with her, however. Instead, you might say: "Sarah, we've tried to fix this problem a number of ways, but we haven't been able to do it. Would you put a team together to come up with a creative way to solve it?"

- A Coach likes to lead a team, but he will be even more motivated if you explain how working together will accomplish two goals: solving the problem and building people.

- The Accountability Partner isn't motivated by creativity, but if you explain how her role of producing and following a prescribed system will help accomplish the goal, she's all in.

Your job is to identify the abilities in these people because they may not see them for themselves!

> We need to value the team as people—not as cogs in the corporate machine—and align their abilities with the company's goals so that we can inspire them to excellence.

Stop Wasting Time

It's vital to help people identify strengths, but some organizational consultants report that it's even more important to help them identify areas in which they *aren't* gifted. Too many people pursue the wrong career for years, and at the end, they've wasted a lot of valuable time. Let me give you a for instance to illustrate what I mean.

> I worked with a young lady—let's call her Catherine—who wanted more than anything in the world to be head of human resources for her company someday. She took courses, attended seminars, spent time with the HR department team, and applied for every position that opened up there. The problem, however, was that Catherine lacked a keen perception about people. Inventories about her personality and abilities that the HR team administered confirmed this time after time, but for four years, Catherine refused to believe it.
>
> She bugged the team so much that finally, in exasperation, they set up a meeting for her with the HR director. He then told her, in no uncertain terms, that she wasn't cut out for the department. Very reluctantly, Catherine shifted her focus back to what she was doing: accounting.
>
> It took her a while to adjust her expectations, but today she's thrilled to be where she is. "What in the world was I thinking?" she said to me. "I don't even pick up on cues from my best friends. Why would I think I'd be terrific in HR?"

So, although it's important to help others see abilities in themselves that they may not see, it's just as important that we be real in the opposite sense. If employees clearly lack abilities that they are certain they possess, it's cowardly to let them continue to suffer under a delusion. It will only lead to profound failure.

I've seen other employees who riveted their desires toward becoming a speaker, a corporate trainer, or a top executive in the company. I'm always wary when someone is ambitious for *position* rather than *impact*. This may seem like too fine a distinction, but I don't think so. At some points in my career, I've thought ambition was a virtue; at other times, I've condemned it as a vice. Ultimately, I've learned that ambition is neutral—it depends on the object of its desires.

I'm always wary when someone is ambitious for *position* rather than *impact*. Ultimately, I've learned that ambition is neutral—it depends on the object of its desires.

When people tell me they want to move up to a top-level position or find a role that gives them a platform from which to be the center of attention, I ask a few more questions. I want to know whether they really care about making a difference, or whether they simply want the power and applause that the position promises. Power and applause—these two temptations can lead good people off track if they're not careful. There's nothing wrong with having powerful positions as long as we don't crave the power in order to dominate people. Similarly, there's nothing wrong with applause if it's a gift from those who appreciate our efforts.

Our motivations become skewed and self-absorbed, though, if we live for positions and approval instead of for influencing and empowering people for *their* sake. And self-absorbed leaders fail convincingly at inspiring their teams. They're wasting their time.

Authentic Thanks

One of the most powerful but often most underutilized management tools is saying a simple "Thanks" to people who have done a good job. Whether you know it or not, a thank-you offered to someone who may not realize that he has a gift or talent can make the lights come on. For that person, it can mean the difference between recognizing his abilities—and being inspired to use them—and staying forever in the dark about what he's good at.

Sometimes, expressing genuine appreciation seems to go even further than money, which is truly amazing when you consider the difficult economic times the world is facing right now. Most companies are not in a position to offer raises, but they can offer praises.

I actually witnessed this principle in play recently when I spoke before a group of HR directors. My host, an executive at a Fortune 100 company, was being "felt out" by a cohort to see if she might be open to jumping ship and working somewhere else for more money. I could tell by her response that she must get this question quite a bit.

"Thanks for your interest," she said. "I am honored you would consider referring me. But what I lack in financial consideration, I more than get back in appreciation from my CEO. I don't take the fact that she is so appreciative for granted." Wow, I remember thinking, I just witnessed how far the currency of appreciation can really go.

So remember: a word of genuine appreciation can make a person's day (or week). It can also illuminate for that individual the skills and personal attributes that he may not have even known he had. And it can cause a team member to see her most mundane task as invaluable to the whole organization. One heartfelt thank-you from you, and suddenly your team's "ordinary" work becomes extraordinary. Your appreciation had better be for real, though. Authentic gratitude is a sweet aroma, but if it seems forced and phony, it stinks.

We don't have to be great communicators to say "Thank you." We just have to mean it. And we can be sure that every person in our world—those up and down the corporate ladder, peers, spouses, children, friends, strangers, and everybody else—will light up when we look them in the eye and say: "Thanks. I really appreciate what you do." This is especially so in situations where they've long forgotten the merit of what they do.

One of the trends among younger workers is a growing thirst for appreciation at work. This demographic loves their freedom and independence, and they aren't attracted to long-term corporate commitments. For them, security comes through relationships, and appreciation seals and lubes those relationships better than anything else. Obviously, then, the more you know about a person's personality type, dreams, and abilities, the more accurately you can frame your words of praise and thanks.

Some time ago, I decided to be more intentional about thanking people and praising their efforts, and it's paid off big time.

- To an analytical person on our team, I said, "Tammy, you did a great job breaking down this complex task into sequential steps so that all of us could understand the critical path and implement the plan."

- To Tim, our team's creative director, I said: "You captured the concept beautifully in your design. Now everyone who sees the image instantly understands what we're trying to communicate."

- To an accountability-oriented team member, I said: "Barbara, you did a fantastic job assessing the cost of the project in terms of human resources. Your contribution made a huge difference to our success."

From the very first time I spoke to each one in this way, the entire mood of our team was transformed. Everybody took off in an incredibly positive direction. Soon, whenever we met, each individual instantly knew the scope and value of the contribution he or she would make, and collectively, they were highly motivated—that is, *inspired*—to excel even more.

GRATITUDE AND THE BOTTOM LINE

In *The Elements of Great Managing*, Rodd Wagner and James K. Harter researched the impact of employee recognition on work performance and productivity. The results were staggering. In companies ranging from health care to banking, when employees felt appreciated they did better work and connected more effectively with clients and customers. The authors observed: "A large multi-company analysis puts the average benefit of such a shift of recognition at 6.5 percent greater productivity and 2 percent higher customer engagement . . . where each percentage point equates to hundreds of millions in sales for a Fortune 500 company." Translation: *thanking employees for their good work makes a difference in the company's bottom line.*

My personality enables me to relate to people very easily, so for years I didn't think I had to try too hard to show appreciation. I was wrong. Being thankful is so important that it deserves at least a few minutes of attention and planning—and we get better with practice. When I began to be more intentional about thanking others by thinking about them for a few minutes before every team meeting, I began noticing more reasons to thank people. And the more I noticed, the more specific I could be. I never want to be phony. I want to notice what people have done to contribute to the success of the team and point it out as authentically as I can. It makes a difference—to them, to me, and to the effectiveness of our team.

To be effective in affirming the abilities of team members, leaders need vision, insight, and the ability to value skills that are different from their own. They need vision to see the whole picture: the corporate and project goals, the contribution of each team member, and how these can work together to be most effective. Leaders need insight into each individual to know how to align his or her personality, motivations, and skills with job functions and responsibilities. And leaders need to be humble enough that they aren't threatened when others have certain talents that surpass their own. Good leaders may be able to perform all of the tasks of every person on the team, but great team leaders develop and inspire people to become more skilled in their individual fields of expertise than they are.

> When I began to be more intentional about thanking others by thinking about them for a few minutes before every team meeting, I began noticing more reasons to thank people. And the more I noticed, the more specific I could be.

When we recognize and affirm others' abilities, they feel empowered, and they take more initiative. Old fears fade, and hesitation evaporates. In place of them arises the freedom for others to be themselves and to contribute powerfully to the team. And as people enjoy using their strengths, managers spend less time trying to pump up their teams and more time on strategically guiding them to be more effective. It's a lot more fun to ride in a car with a powerful engine that's running on all cylinders than to have to push a tired car uphill. Yet too many managers have been pushing their teams so long that they're all exhausted and resentful. It doesn't have to be that way. Every team member whose strengths are recognized, validated, and appreciated by the manager is far more likely to be a powerful piston in the machine. So be smart. Fill their tanks with praise.

In the chapter about Principle 2 (Connect with Others' Dreams), we discussed the importance of noticing, naming, and nurturing others' dreams. As you can see from this chapter, it's equally important to apply these *same* actions with regard to people's abilities. The spirit of an inspired team is your company's *most valuable* intangible asset, but it's an asset you will never own if you don't take the time to affirm your team members.

- *Notice* the abilities that they can't see in themselves.
- *Name* them, in private and in front of others.
- *Nurture* their skills so that everybody on the team becomes an integral—and successful—part of a well-oiled machine.

It's the only way to inspire.

GET INSPIRED—SEE IN OTHERS THE ABILITIES THEY DON'T SEE IN THEMSELVES

Outcome Objectives for Weeks Five and Six

You will be able to align what you believe are your strengths and potential with what your circle of colleagues, friends, and family believe are your strengths and potential.

Equipping Yourself

1. Register for the 360 Profile at Inspirationblvd.com and follow the directions for inviting the appropriate people to participate.
2. Enlist someone you trust to share the results of your 360 Profile with. Look for consensus about your strengths and weaknesses.

Inspiring Others

1. Encourage your team to also participate in the 360 Profile.

2. Set aside some time in either a team retreat or an extended team meeting to talk about the findings.

GOING DEEPER

Enlist someone you trust to serve as a coach to help create a plan for developing your potential in the area of your strengths and working around your weaknesses.

Speak with Credibility

The most tragic thing in the world is a man of genius who is not a man of honor.
—George Bernard Shaw, Irish playwright, literary critic, essayist

ACCORDING TO *Merriam-Webster's Collegiate Dictionary* (eleventh edition), *credibility* is the "quality or power of inspiring belief." Just as psychologists and neuroscientists in recent history have identified different types of intelligence—emotional, spatial, linguistic, and musical, among others—credibility, too, can be broken down into different categories. In this chapter, I examine the five main types of credibility and apply them to your role as someone who motivates and inspires others. The principle I most want to convey here is what I refer to as "moral authority." In other words, you can lead only where you have first gone, and your credibility allows you to do so without ever saying "You can trust me."

What's our reaction to a person who says, "Trust me"? Our gut reflex is to do the exact opposite—not to trust him. The fact is there is a direct correlation between our credibility and our trustworthiness. Our credibility never needs to be flaunted; it needs to be lived out. When our lives *demonstrate* our credibility, we will no doubt have an exalting influence on another's heart, mind, and will. When times of stress and difficulties come, people will always seek out those who have credibility for inspiration. Inspiration is not expected from those with no credibility, even if their title insinuates they are the "boss."

Types of Credibility

Credibility, in essence, is a blend of several important ingredients that convincingly communicate to others this message: "I've been there. I know what I'm talking about, and I know what you're going through. When I offer to help, you can trust me." Let's look at the various types of credibility you can master that will allow you to speak with such authority.

INTELLECTUAL CREDIBILITY

In today's society, we are often impressed by a person's résumé and the degrees listed there. At the same time, though, we instinctively realize that one's intellect goes far beyond a list of letters after his or her name. Some of the greatest leaders, such as Abraham Lincoln, were self-taught. They had nimble, open, inquisitive minds, and they earned the right to be heard because of their wealth of *experience*. But whether their knowledge comes from the classroom or the "school of hard knocks," the people we respect are those who know what they're talking about—especially if they don't try to impress and bowl us over with their credentials. Such people possess *intellectual credibility*. They aren't threatened by others' questions, so they answer them with honesty. If they don't know the answer, they admit it and do whatever it takes to find it.

One of the common traits of all people with intellectual credibility is their commitment to reading. I will always be grateful to Jon Wiggington for entering my life early on in my career. He was an enthusiastic and dedicated reader of everything he could get his hands on about leadership. We'd meet once a week for an early breakfast and Jon would already have been there thirty minutes before I arrived, reading and underlining. I was inspired not by how much he knew but by his hunger to learn from others. Jon taught me in those meetings how to create a reading plan based on my interests and passions. I have followed his system for twenty-plus years of reading: one book on leadership, followed by one book on spiritual growth, followed by one novel.

I realize that all readers are not necessarily leaders, but I am confident that all leaders are serious readers. Here's a prime example. I recently met with Karen Pettoruto, one of the trainers at Phillips Medical. It really did not take long to see why she was so successful in what she did. As with most inspiring leaders, she immediately began to share with me what she was learning from some of her recent readings. Karen pulled out her Kindle and in response to my request, went through a list of some fifty books she had read over the previous year. What was more impressive, however, was how she could pull thoughts and insights from so many discrete sources. It was a reminder to me that if we will just keep making deposits into our intellectual bank account, we will always be ready to share at the appropriate time.

Having intellectual credibility also requires us to accept the fact that even though we might read deep and wide, there is still a lot more we don't know than what we do know. I recall a conversation I had with an individual who referred to himself as an "intellectual atheist." I had never met anyone who identified himself this way, and I thought the label a rather interesting oxymoron.

"Of all the things there are to know in the world, what percentage of those things would you say you actually know?" I asked.

His response clearly revealed just how good he felt about himself: "Fifty percent."

"Wow . . . that's huge! Even so, if you assume you know 50 percent of all there is to know, there is still another 50 percent to be known. And is there a chance that God is part of that 50 percent you don't yet know?"

Having intellectual credibility also means you know when to share what you know and when not to speak at all. Have you ever noticed that there always seems to be one person in every training session who knows more than anyone else and has read more than anyone else? Maybe such men and women really do know more and have read more, but the fact that they just wear you out with all that they know causes them to lose what intellectual credibility they may have had.

MORAL CREDIBILITY

Too often in our culture we tolerate destructive behavior in ourselves and are entertained by the sins of others. In this environment, a truly moral person stands out tall and strong. She rejects deceit and corruption. She treasures honesty and decency. She is a person of *moral credibility*.

Morally credible people don't flaunt their purity; nor do they delight in condemning those who fail. Instead, they befriend the fallen, just as Christ did. He was a true "friend of sinners" (see Matthew 11:19 and Luke 7:34). Even those whose morals were rocky knew that Jesus loved and accepted them. And his gracious, unpretentious love, coupled with his uncompromised morals, made him eternally credible. As such, Christ inspired and changed many lives—including mine.

I am always reluctant to hold up any one person as the ultimate example of being morally credible for two reasons: first, no one is perfect, and second, as soon as I do, that individual becomes a target for the media to discredit. Yet, I am powerfully moved by a number of businesspeople who have withstood the temptation to paint with the color gray. As I share with you the story of one of them, I hope that it will inspire you to become intentional about leading with moral credibility.

Meet Jon M. Huntsman Sr., businessman and philanthropist. I myself had the honor of meeting this gentleman at his own surprise birthday party. Many of his friends had gathered to honor him and his incredible personal vision and quest to help find a cure for cancer. Most people recognize his name as that of a member of a very elite group of Americans—namely, the "billionaire club." What many may not know is that Jon Sr. spent a short period of time as the White House staff secretary and special assistant to the president during Richard Nixon's first term in office.

In his book *Winners Never Cheat*, Jon Sr. revealed that, as part of H. R. Haldeman's so-called staff, he was expected to be loyal to the president without question. On one occasion, when he was asked to "help" the president of the United States, he was, in actuality, being asked to do something that violated his moral values. "There are times when we react too quickly to catch the rightness and wrongness of something immediately," Jon Sr. wrote. "This was one of those times. It took fifteen minutes for my moral compass to make itself noticed. Values that had accompanied me since childhood kicked in."

I can say with confidence that the values Jon M. Huntsman Sr. wrote about in his book are the very values he runs his business by to this day. The Huntsman Cancer Center in Salt Lake City is one of my premier clients and a shining light to so many who are tempted to run their personal lives in one silo and their business lives in another. How do I know? The founder's values and his commitment to integrity are evident in the lives of his team members. They are self-sacrificing, compassionate, serving, hardworking individuals who do not struggle with what's right and what's wrong. When your business is asking people for large sums of money, you never want to have to explain moral hiccups and failures.

RELATIONAL CREDIBILITY

Most of the time, we know who is trustworthy and who should be tested again before we trust them. Those we choose to trust fully are typically those individuals who possess *relational credibility*, that is, repute they've earned based on their relationships with us. Relational credibility doesn't produce blind loyalty; rather, loyalty grows out of a person's reputation for telling the truth and doing so in a way that is most helpful to the hearer. People who demonstrate relational credibility never use people; on the contrary, they have our best interests at heart, and we know it.

When I think of people who exude relational credibility, my friend Victor Oliver is top on my list. Victor is an executive at a major publishing company, and for the last five years, I've spent time with him in business meetings, at coffee shops, on the golf course, and in every other conceivable situation. I've watched him relate to corporate executives, and I've seen him interact with punk rock–loving, Gothic baristas. In every encounter, Victor gives each individual undistracted attention. His demeanor, eye contact, and words communicate, "You are important to me." People sense it, and they instantly trust him. I've seen tears well up in people's eyes simply because Victor communicated grace to them. Perhaps he's the only one who has demonstrated that he truly cares, and they soak it up, suddenly unafraid to show their emotions. Why? Because in every relationship, be it close or casual, it is clear that he is *genuine*. Above all things, Victor is a man of truth. In fact, he has said some hard things to me that I wouldn't have accepted from anyone else. And I listened.

Truth and grace: these are the mark of Victor Oliver—and of *anyone* with relational credibility.

EMOTIONAL CREDIBILITY

We earn respect when we are honest with ourselves about the full range of our emotions and appropriately communicate them to others. Many people are afraid of losing control of their explosive feelings, so they keep the lid on tight, increasing the pressure and producing an even bigger explosion later. On the other hand, some people express more emotions than others care to know about! They wear their feelings on their sleeves—and on our sleeves too.

But those who are balanced, controlling and suitably sharing their emotions, demonstrate *emotional credibility*. We trust them because they are on an even keel. We're not fearful of sudden, unpredictable outbursts or random displays of emotion. Emotionally credible people are even-tempered, but they're also honest about their anger, hurts, doubts, fears, and dreams, and they inspire us to be honest about ours.

> We earn respect when we are honest with ourselves about the full range of our emotions and appropriately communicate them to others.

Emotional credibility is not a personality trait; neither is it skewed by ethnicity. It is simply a matter of disciplining our wills to rule over our emotions. This story about my great client and friend Sandra illustrates exactly what I mean.

Sandra has been working in the same environment, and basically at the same level, for more than five years now. I am personally familiar with her work, and it is excellent. Yet she has watched many of her associates pass her by for promotions and new opportunities that she was better qualified to handle.

One day while we were at lunch together, she mentioned that she was aware of an upcoming meeting that I had scheduled with her boss. She then asked me to please find a tactful way of asking him why she was seemingly being slighted in favor of others. I told her I would do so on one condition: "That you be willing to hear, receive, and adjust to whatever I learn, if anything." She agreed.

When I finally met with her boss, at some point I broached the subject. "You know, I really enjoy working with Sandra. She is quite intuitive when it comes to tracking and reporting. She must really like what she does in that position, because she has been there ever since I first started working with you."

The boss was more than willing to talk about it. "I like Sandra a lot," he confided, "and she does outstanding work. Unfortunately, she has made some real enemies, not by what she says but how she goes about saying it. She has a hard time keeping her emotions under control when someone disagrees with her. She feels like she always has to be right."

Based on Sandra's commitment to hear whatever was said, I made it a point to sit down and share with her what I had learned. Before I offered any details about my conversation with her boss, however, I challenged her to be open and coachable. Her assurance given, I then proceeded to share her boss's perception in the context of how she can get ahead.

"Sandra, you are recognized as being a wonderful talent, and your hard work is noticed and very much appreciated. What seems to be holding you back is the perception that you are not open to the ideas of others. You are perceived as being defensive because you talk as if you always have to be right when others disagree with you."

Sandra's response to me affirmed her boss's perception. "So, do I just not say anything even though I feel so strongly about it?"

I encouraged her to demonstrate how she could be open to others' ideas by saying something like this: "I hadn't considered that perspective. Thank you for sharing it. I think I can find a way to incorporate your idea into what I am doing."

Sandra paused and did her best to process what she was hearing. I could tell this was an entirely new way of thinking and talking for her. She came back with: "But to not say something in my *own* way would be fake of me. I'm just a passionate person. My entire family is this way."

Bringing the conversation back to her objective, to advance her career, I said: "I am not suggesting that you be anything other than who you are. What I am suggesting, though, is that if you want to be an inspiring individual with great influence, you will have to tell your feelings to yield to your objectives, not the other way around."

By her own admission this was going to be a challenge: to begin to speak out for the greater good of the organization and not simply based upon what she "felt" needed to be said. In due time it paid off. Sandra was promoted to another position within six months after she began to put her thinking in charge of her emotions.

Here are some practical ways to keep your emotions in check and help you live with emotional credibility. These will also be spelled out as part of your twelve-week plan for creating an inspiring culture.

- Believe the best about the people you work with. If you don't like the emotions you are feeling, change what you believe. For example, if you believe "they are out to get you," you are going to feel paranoid. If you believe you are "purposefully being kept out of the loop," you are going to feel insignificant. Choose to think the best and it will yield a more positive emotion. Realize there is a difference between your interpretation and what just may be the truth.

- Use e-mail to communicate facts, not feelings. I love this one. Have you ever noticed that e-mail can be abrupt even when you don't mean for it to be? How much more abrupt is it when you *do* mean for it to be? If you are communicating just the facts anyway,

YOU REALLY DON'T NEED ALL CAPS, RED INK, AND EXCLAMATION POINTS!!!!

- When in a confrontational meeting, focus on the problem and not the people with the problem.

- Choose in advance how you want your colleagues to think of you. You can be your own best friend by preparing your mind before a meeting. Do you want your associates to recall you as enthusiastic, reflective, and a creative problem solver, or as someone they have to be guarded around? This is powerful because it is, simply, your choice.

EXPERIENTIAL CREDIBILITY

It would be easy to address experiential credibility if all it meant was a good track record. No doubt about it, that speaks volumes, especially when an organization is caught up in the fray of internal politics, external market pressure, and lots of economic uncertainty. (I think I just summarized the "state of the union" for corporate America without meaning to.)

Many times, though, a proven track record can be gained simply by delivering the bottom line—without regard to the human "casualties" along the way. Let me use the experience of a dear friend, Cal, who served as COO for a midsize oil company, to show how this can play out in a boardroom.

At the height of the oil spike, when oil was selling in excess of $140 a barrel, this company was bleeding red ink. Why? Many reasons, but above all, several of the board members had a conflict of interest with some of the competing oil companies, who were all bidding to push oil through the same pipelines. Making a competitive bid would have cost them money on their other interests, which were obviously greater than their interest in this corporation. Thus, there was significant self-induced disparity regarding the forecast for the year. The answer? Cut costs.

Many companies have had to deal with cutbacks, and they are never pleasant. But to add insult to injury in this case, a blackball process had been devised to determine who would stay and who would go. When the communication plan unfolded, everyone who was blackballed was invited to a "very important mandatory meeting" off-site. The survivors were then sent a separate notice inviting them to show up at the same time for a very different kind of meeting. You see where this is going.

A week after all of this unfolded, Cal, bothered by the way it all came down, walked into his CEO's office and shared with conviction that though he had appreciated his tenure, he was at a crossroads with his personal conscience and the company's values. And because he was unable to square them in his mind, he resigned, without knowing where he was going next. To me, that's inspiring.

The story is not quite over, because the principle of experiential credibility was about to pay off for him. Cal went without a job for about six months; then a large company actively recruited him. Yes, he had a good track record, but so did lots of other candidates. He had great credentials, but again, so did many others. But when this company offered him the job, they told him that above all of those other reasons, they wanted him because they had heard about why he had left his previous job.

Experiential credibility communicates the strong message "I can do the job, I have the firsthand experience," with a thread of integrity running through it. Experience alone can say simply, "I have the know-how for this position." But experiential credibility adds, "*and* I will deliver what I promise without cutting corners or walking on others."

These traits form a matrix of credibility, but none of us gets a 10 out of 10 in all categories. King David was an incredible military commander with astute political instincts, but his moral failures crippled his reign. General Robert E. Lee has been idolized for generations, yet he was too dominating in the lives of his daughters.

Even so, both men successfully inspired those around them. You can do the same, and you don't have to be perfect to do so. You just have to be, as best you can, a person others can *believe* in. You'll make mistakes, and in some areas your credibility may be tarnished. But if others see you, by and large, as a person of *integrity*, then the good in you will serve as inspiration to those who need your example. Here's the story of a CEO who learned precisely that in real life.

A few years ago, I served as a consultant for a large ad agency in the Midwest. The CEO was a very bright guy who had tremendous business savvy, but rumors leaked out about his handling of company finances. Like many CEOs, he used promotions and bonuses to reward his favorite VPs, but the problem was that the bonuses didn't seem to have any correlation with performance. That raised suspicion, especially among the VPs who received less than they felt they deserved. As always, unmet expectations soon led to resentment.

Not long after that, the company experienced financial difficulties, but another rumor leaked out: though no bonuses would be paid to any of the employees, both the CEO and the CFO received hefty checks. Suspicion and resentment then escalated to deep distrust and outright rebellion.

The company continued to experience problems, and they had to be downsized. Several of the VPs who felt their unscrupulous CEO had cheated them out of their rightful bonuses took this opportunity to resign and start new companies. Some of these companies became chief competitors and almost drove the original company out of business.

In this case, a leader's selfishness and financial mismanagement created such bad blood that it severely crippled the company. To this day, the company has never recovered. The CEO ended up being escorted by a member of his board out of his own office. Not even his multiplied talent, salesmanship, and inside connections could cover the overdraft of trust that his lack of moral credibility created.

I recently ran into this man in an airport and had the opportunity to talk with him about those days. Pain will teach you much if you let it, and he had allowed his pain to do exactly that. In the few minutes we shared together, he told me about how his discipline and good judgment just got away from him. "Things were moving so fast and we were making so much money," he said, "that I just didn't take time to adjust to my moral conscience until it was too late. Now I spend the first fifteen minutes of every day in the book of Proverbs, aligning my compass."

I'm very happy for him. Unfortunately, for his former employer, however, it was too little, too late.

How do things like this happen to those who at one time were decent people with good reputations? In the case of this CEO, he had surrounded himself with people who would only say yes. He had built a system that had insulated him from any form of accountability. That's a very scary place for any of us to be in. Why? Because we are all capable of compromising our credibility. The first step toward such a compromise seems to be a lack of accountability. We all need someone to do life with whom we can trust to always speak the truth to us no matter how much it hurts. We all need someone we can be accountable to. And the more successful we become, the more we need such a person.

Several years ago now, I actually met with the infamous televangelist Jim Bakker. At the time he was living alone in a house that was being loaned to him by a friend. On the walls were all the familiar pictures of him with some of the most famous people in the world. In our brief time together, he talked about what he had learned in prison and that ultimately led to a glimpse of what went wrong. No need for the detail, because he made all that very clear in his autobiography, *I Was Wrong*. But suffice it to say that he had clearly made the same mistake as the ad agency CEO had. He surrounded himself with only yes-men and yes-women and insulated himself from the very people who would have and could have been a good source of healthy accountability. The result was a compromise in credibility.

The Cost of a Credibility Deficit

The lack of credibility affects corporate America in many different ways, from the impact of elevated staff stress levels to the increased costs of doing business that have resulted from new federal regulations enacted to prevent mismanagement. After the Enron debacle, for instance, Congress passed the Sarbanes-Oxley Act of 2002 to clamp down on corporate fraud.

If you think that didn't cost corporate America, consider this: According to Stephen M. R. Covey in *The Speed of Trust*, "the cost of implementing one section [of Sarbanes-Oxley] alone [was] $35 billion, exceeding the original SEC estimates by 28 times." These costs, of course, will be passed along to consumers—and all because of the lack of corporate credibility. In fact, says Covey, *any time* trust deteriorates, the speed of business slows down and costs increase, a phenomenon he calls the "trust tax."

What about the costs on the home front? When parents lose credibility *at home*, what can they expect? Going back to the dictionary definition of credibility, once parents squander their "power of inspiring belief," they begin to lose power of *every* kind. What do I mean?

Parents are wasting their breath when they tell their children not to smoke even as they themselves light up. If they wanted to inspire their teens to be nonsmokers, they just failed. Similarly, when mom and dad barely make it home from the party without taking out five other vehicles, yet they tell their own son not to drink, oh, they inspire him all right—to rebel. And parents who want to motivate their children to be honest will never succeed when they themselves play loose with the facts.

In all three cases, not only has the power to inspire belief been lost, the power to persuade *in general* has been compromised. Parents, at every point where our children notice a disconnect between our words and our actions, our credibility gap widens. The price? We lose their respect. We risk disobedience and even open rebellion. And their confidence in our word may never be restored. Where once we could *inspire*, we now have to *compel*. This is a lack of moral authority. It's a high price to pay for not being credible.

> Parents, at every point where our children notice a disconnect between our words and our actions, our credibility gap widens.

If, on the other hand, our children observe that we "walk the talk," that is, our words and our actions are consistent, we build credibility, and we inspire our children. Dad, your son and daughter will say, "I want to be *just like you.*" Mom, your daughter and son will begin to mimic every good quality they see in you. Your children have rung up your words on the cash register of their experience and accepted them as *credible*. They will not hesitate to follow your example. And speaking of example . . .

CREDIBILITY CAN BE GAINED THROUGH SERVANT LEADERSHIP

A few months ago, I was in a meeting in Nashville with Dan Cathy, the son of Truett Cathy, founder of Chick-fil-A. Dan is now the president and COO of the very successful company, and it's not hard to see why.

The day we met, Dan did something few executives would ever do. As our party began getting into a van to go to a meeting, we discovered that there wasn't quite enough room for everybody. Instantly, Dan jumped out, saying only, "Take my seat," to the person standing outside. Dan then walked to the back of the van and got in with the luggage. He didn't make a big deal of it. There was no image he was trying to project or protect. Dan was just being himself. He lives to serve others, and this was simply one moment among many of selfless service in a lifestyle of caring for others.

Do people around him notice? You bet. Are they affected? Profoundly. Leaders should never expect people to do anything they themselves aren't willing to do. Dan doesn't. He is more than willing to do anything that he asks his employees to do—and they know it. I wonder how many people will be inspired to imitate his actions in the years to come.

Trust is a precious but fragile commodity. Where it grows in relationships, people experience the wonderful blend of contentment and zeal, but where it is eroded, stress levels rise and suspicions rule, both at the office and at home. We simply can't inspire people who don't trust us. We may be able to control them, but we can't truly inspire them.

To review, any leader, whether of a corporation or a houseful of teenagers, earns the right to speak by being trustworthy in the five key areas we just examined:

- Intellectual Credibility: When people trust our intellect, they'll be inspired to listen when we make personal or professional recommendations.

- Moral Credibility: When they trust our morals, others are showing that they know our motives are pure. We're not "out to get them"; instead, we've got their best interests at heart.

- Relational Credibility: When the people we lead are confident in their relationship with us, they're unafraid to step out and take progressive actions.

- Emotional Credibility: If we have demonstrated emotional stability, others won't constantly be operating in a second-guess mode: *What if I make a mistake? Will she blow her top? Will I get fired? Will he pick someone else?* That's hardly a recipe for inspiration.

- Experiential Credibility: When we can point to hard-won experience, those we lead are confident that we know what we're talking about. To follow our lead, then, is natural, not contrived.

We can never demand that people trust us. We earn the right to be believed, one moment at a time—at home, at the coffee shop, on the warehouse floor, in the boardroom, or in a van on the way to a meeting. All day, every day, we have countless opportunities to either build or erode our credibility with the people around us.

Which will you choose to do?

GET INSPIRED—SPEAK WITH CREDIBILITY

Outcome Objectives for Week Seven

- You will be able to describe five types of credibility.
- You will be able to share with others how to monitor your decisions based on your moral compass.
- You will be able to list the markings of a servant leader.

Equipping Yourself

1. Who are some people (write in code here) you thought of at first as trustworthy, but later on you found out they were not? How did you feel around each of these persons before the revelation? After it?

2. Give yourself a score of 0 (abysmal) to 10 (you *are* the model) in these areas of credibility:
    _____ Intellectual
    _____ Moral
    _____ Relational
    _____ Emotional
    _____ Experiential
    Which type or types are you strong in? Which do you need to improve in? What will you do about it?

3. A former CEO talked about how he spends time reading the book of Proverbs every morning as a way of making sure he is following his moral compass. What are some other ways you would suggest to accomplish the same thing?

4. One way to make sure you are following your moral compass is to enlist a trusted friend to hold you accountable. Who in your life could you select as an accountability partner? What areas of your life would you like more accountability in?

5. Dan Cathy illustrated what a servant-leader does in just one simple way. What would be other ways you would recognize a servant-leader?

Inspiring Others

Being self-righteous is very different from being credible. What's the difference between the two terms? How do you maintain being credible without coming across as self-righteous?

GOING DEEPER

Make a list of high profile cases such as Tyco, Enron, Worldcom. (There is quite an infamous list if you were to Google "corporate fraud.") See if you can discover these three insights from studying them:

• Where did they first begin to go wrong?

• What do they all have in common?

• What can you learn from them and apply to your own life and situation?

Tell Great Stories— Yours and Others'

*You have to understand, my dears, that the shortest distance
between truth and a human being is a story.*
—Anthony de Mello, Indian psychotherapist, Jesuit priest, author

"STORY," WROTE AUTHOR and educator Jim Trelease, "is the vehicle we use to make sense of our lives in a world that often defies logic."

Ah, stories. We love them. Nothing can capture our hearts like a good story. It should come as no surprise, then, that the most inspiring people in history were those who told gripping stories. Four of my favorites are Abraham Lincoln, Mark Twain, Ronald Reagan, and Jesus Christ—not necessarily in that order. Whatever we may think of their personal lives or their politics, these men had an impact on millions . . . by telling *stories*.

Skillfully woven stories often become the fodder for blockbuster movies. And what makes them blockbusters instead of B movies is their ability to move us. Some of their story lines move us to anger, others to melancholy, and still others to frivolity. Some of us are stirred by the courage of the men in *Black Hawk Down*; others of us are inspired by the love and loyalty of the sisters in *Sense and Sensibility*.

Although we may differ from other people in the movies we each prefer, at the core, we *all* gravitate toward those with story lines that touch our hearts, and we remember them. We may forget our first-grade teacher's name, what we wore on our first date—even what we had for dinner last night—but we will never forget a meaningful story told well. In fact, when people have long forgotten *my* name, they'll remember the stories I told them. Why? Because there's power in story. If you are a great inspirer, you already know this.

The Power of Stories

Great leaders tell great stories. They understand that stories are among their greatest resources for inspiring those under them. Sometimes they craft and communicate their own tales. At other times, they draw on the experiences of others. But either way, a great leader telling a great story will touch hearts and change lives.

A meaningful story can make the difference between a boring meeting and one that team members eagerly anticipate, between an ineffective teacher-student conference and a productive one, between a father-son talk that works and one that doesn't. Sadly, many people either don't understand the power of stories or don't expend the effort to craft them for the people they lead.

STORYTELLING WORKS

Stories can be used effectively in virtually every context, with or without props or visual aids. Further, you don't have to be a master communicator to tell effective stories. You simply have to tell stories that capture *your* interest and motivate *you*. If you're moved by it, then it's likely that you'll tell the story in a way that moves others. It's that simple.

People who inspire others tell stories to

- Teach life lessons.
- Keep important traditions alive.
- Say hard-to-hear things.
- Share vision.
- Rally a team together.
- Connect with the soul of another person or even the soul of an audience.

Tell stories that capture *your* interest and motivate *you*. If you're moved by it, then it's likely that you'll tell the story in a way that moves others.

Some people, though, won't even try. They hide behind the excuse that they're not "gifted" speakers. But if you have a pulse, you can be an effective storyteller. It may be rough at first, but just as you refine any other ability, you can improve your storytelling skills. You know the cliché: Practice makes perfect. As you learn the craft, you'll find that particular types of stories fit your personality better than others do and that you enjoy telling certain stories more than others. Ultimately, you'll develop an entire repertoire of stories to tell at appropriate times to reinforce certain points, and you'll always be hunting for more stories that you can use to inspire people around you.

I was recently invited to present our seminar on corporate parables in Michigan. The objective of this seminar is to teach people how to use the element of story to connect with employees and customers. Without a doubt, it's my favorite among all of the seminars my company offers because it transcends personalities, cultures, and even talent. (As part of your twelve-week plan, you will be asked to incorporate the element of parables into team meetings and other corporate gatherings.) The story that follows perfectly illustrates this point.

A man who identified himself as an Accountability Partner came to me during the break in a cold sweat. "If this is one of those public speech things," he sputtered, "I will need to excuse myself." I asked if he could sit down with me for a moment, and he agreed. We each got something to drink and found a couple of seats, away from other participants. He then told me his name was Samuel.

"Do you have children, Samuel?" I asked.

"Yes," he said, and proceeded to tell me that his children were sixteen, ten, and six years old.

"When they were small, did you read stories to them?"

With a faraway and blissful look in his eye, Samuel sighed and said, "Yes. Their favorite book, bar none, was *The Giving Tree*."

Perfect! I thought. I was very familiar with this controversial children's book, written in 1964 by Shel Silverstein. "Ah . . . great book," I said. "Hey, do you remember the lesson behind the story?"

"Of course," Samuel answered. "If you give, you will always get back."

"Well, did you ever once have to explain that moral to your children after you read them the book?" I pressed.

He answered no.

"Why?"

"Well," he replied, a little flustered now, "because the lesson was clear. It needed no explanation."

"Samuel," I said, "what I am proposing in this seminar is that you find a story, and hopefully many stories, you can share with the people you supervise that will instill the noble corporate values this company so firmly believes in."

"That's it?" he said. "You just want me to tell a *story* to my team?"

Yes, that's it! Likewise, I want you, reader, to learn how to harness the element of story to make your point every day, every way. Our brains are hardwired to receive stories, not facts and figures. Sure, information is necessary; statistics provide quantification. But *story* provides meaning and relevance.

Which means more to you: the *fact* that 269,800 American women will die of breast cancer in the next twelve months, or the *story* about your wife or your mother or your sister who just might be a statistic? You get the point.

This same principle applies in industry, every industry. People are not moved to action by "data"; they are moved by story.

From ancient times, history was kept alive by oral tradition. When the early church began installing stained glass windows, it was more than just an aesthetic move. It was a way to transcend languages and cultures through beautiful, ornate glass panels that depicted a story.

Finding a Story

I firmly believe that every person I meet has a great story to tell. In fact, most people have lots of them. I often go exploring. Once I know people in more than a superficial way, I ask each of them to tell me about the path of his or her life's journey. I don't pry. I just ask a simple question or two, and in many cases, great stories tumble out. Some people have thought long and hard about the lessons they've learned from failures, rejection, illness, and other heartbreaking circumstances. They've already done the work of reflection, and the lessons they've discovered shape every aspect of their lives. They can now use this wisdom to inspire others.

But occasionally, right in the middle of telling me their stories, it suddenly dawns on them what they were meant to learn from their experiences. In more than a few serendipitous instances, people's eyes have lit up as they pensively drew the most important conclusions of their lives from the stories they had *just recounted*. And from that moment on, those conclusions became sources of inspiration for all who knew them.

So, what's your story? And more important, how can you tell it so that it inspires someone else?

CRAFT YOUR OWN STORIES

The same things that make the story lines of major motion pictures work apply to our own stories as well. Like any edge-of-your-seat movie, our lives are in constant motion. They aren't static, unbroken lines of sameness. In our pasts, we have each encountered turning points, moments when we came face-to-face with difficult decisions, and the choices we made determined the course of our lives. Some of these were the natural stages that everyone experiences: college and career choices; geographical or professional moves; and births, marriages, and deaths. At other times, though, we faced unexpected (and unwanted) circumstances that tested our values and courage.

Ironically, such defining moments—ones that stopped us in our tracks and caused us to reevaluate our direction in life—filled our lives with possibility. Perhaps we didn't make great decisions at the outset. We stumbled through doubts, depression, fatigue, and failure, but in the end, we found fresh springs of hope. From weakness sprang strength; from failure, success; from rejection, love; and from discouragement, the will to go on. Today these stories define us and give us a wonderful platform from which to inspire others. In fact, *all* difficult events in our lives, even those that didn't turn out well, can be powerfully inspiring if we can find a "moral" or two in them and convey those hard-won lessons through the power of story.

The paragraphs that follow contain tips for how you can fashion great stories that will inspire those around you.

First, examine your own life.

Most of us think our lives are dull and boring, but they aren't. We just need a little effort to remember details and dig for lessons learned. Look through old annuals, scrapbooks, or photo albums. The images will jog your memory and remind you of events long forgotten but rich with lessons you learned—or that you should have learned. Talk to those who were with you during those times to make sure you have your facts straight and ask them to offer insights that you may have missed.

Think about the happiest times in your life, but don't focus only on that which was good. Experiences both positive and negative are the stuff of life, and often, those experiences that were the very worst ultimately led to what was best for each of us. So also reflect on periods of hardship, sickness, and loss. Then, as you narrate, let your listeners feel your pain. Milk the moments when you had no idea what to do next, when all hope seemed lost, when there was seemingly no light at the end of the tunnel, when the situation was less than ideal. See, great stories aren't based on the superficial image of an ideal life; they depict our heroic choices to face reality and find hope instead of despair.

Look for great stories everywhere you go.
We develop habits to reinforce the things we believe are important, and looking for inspiring stories can be like any other habit we cultivate. If you know you need a story to use with your team or family, you'll have your antennae up. When you read the newspaper, you'll notice stories of courage, creativity, endurance, or stupidity. You'll listen to Garrison Keillor on the radio or read books that have gripping narratives. You'll ask people to tell you about the funniest points or the pivotal moments in their lives. You'll write down important stories, you'll clip them out of the newspaper, and you'll copy them from the Internet. (You can find many riveting stories to inspire you, your team, and your family at inspirationblvd.com. Look under "Teachable Moments.")

Make sure your story has a point.
A truly inspirational story communicates a lesson that inspires or warns. Sometimes the lesson is intuitively obvious, but in a few cases, we have to dig a little deeper to find a richer vein of meaning.

Here's a brief story to inspire you. It's about one of my own inspirational heroes, Branch Rickey of the Brooklyn Dodgers. Take a moment to read it, and see if you can identify the life lesson in this story just as you did in the story about Oprah Winfrey.

A truly inspirational story communicates a lesson that inspires or warns.

Branch Rickey is best known for opening the door into baseball for African Americans, but few people know that his character had a profound impact on everyone who knew him. Just being in his presence changed people's lives.

From the very formation of the National League in 1876, team owners and general managers of Major League Baseball had refused to recruit black players, and they were unanimous in their commitment to keep it that way—until Branch Rickey, general manager for the Brooklyn Dodgers, came along.

In the summer of 1945, Rickey sent his chief scout to Chicago to look at a black prospect named Jackie Robinson. Impressed, the scout brought Robinson to New York to meet with Rickey. The two men had a frank discussion about what it would take for Robinson to be the first of his race to play in the major leagues. Sure, Rickey could clearly see Robinson's phenomenal athletic abilities, but beyond that, he saw what was even more critical: the tenacity, wisdom, and discipline to endure the abuse that would be inevitable for the first black player. Rickey offered Jackie a contract, and he signed it. He would play his first season for the Dodgers' top minor-league club, the Montreal Royals. If he did well, he would be brought up to the majors the following year.

In the '46 season, Robinson excelled and led the Royals to the championship of the Minor League World Series. In the spring of '47, Rickey planned to move Robinson up to the Dodgers. To introduce him to the players, he scheduled an exhibition series between the Royals and the Dodgers.

But the Dodger players despised the upstart black man. When they heard rumors that Rickey planned to move him up to join their team, three players wrote a petition and circulated it among the rest of the team. The petition said that the signers demanded to be traded to avoid having to play ball with a black man.

Rickey stood his ground, and Robinson joined the team. Throughout the next decade, Robinson starred in every phase of the game, even though he had to put up with taunts, slurs, and threats from opposing players and fans in every stadium across the country. Nonetheless, in the end, Branch Rickey's moral compass changed the course of baseball and left an indelible imprint on the national culture, and his spiritual courage enabled him to endure vicious opposition from demanding people.

When Rickey died in December 1965, thousands of admirers attended his funeral. Among them was Bobby Bragan, one of the three players who had written the 1947 petition to keep Robinson off the team. Over the years, Bragan had gradually come to realize that Mr. Rickey's decision had changed people's lives, including his own. When a reporter asked Bragan why he had come to the funeral, he replied, "I came because Branch Rickey made me a better man."

What did you learn from this story? Did it affect you? Can you craft a tale that will have a similar effect on your listeners? What experiences do you have that could be the basis for a compelling and inspiring story? Don't rush through this chapter. Take time to be observant, reflective, and insightful. Approach every experience as a possible story to retell, with a lesson to be learned. Inspirationblvd.com was created for the very purpose of gathering stories from which people could glean life lessons that inspire.

Focus on the main points, and deliver the punch line boldly and clearly.
We've all heard speakers ramble on as they told detail after detail of a story that seemed to go on for eternity. At first, we were interested, because all stories promise a meaningful ending, but after a while, boredom killed our hopes. In informal settings, stories don't need a lot of preparation, but if you are speaking to an audience or you plan to use a story multiple times, craft it carefully. Know in advance the first line you want to say, and deliver it as you stand up instead of thanking everyone for being there. Just tell your story and what can be learned and applied from it.

After your strong start, keep your story flowing as you make your main points, adding colorful details to make the tale come alive. Push your listeners' "hot buttons" as you narrate. Remember, you are endeavoring to inspire them. By now you should know some of their dreams and goals. How can your story speak to those aspirations? Look for ways to direct your story to their innermost yearnings.

And don't forget the element of surprise. Great stories inevitably contain one, something that brings us to the edge of our seats. In *Mystery and Manners*, a collection of essays selected and edited by Sally and Robert Fitzgerald, novelist Flannery O'Connor reflects:

> From my own experience in trying to make stories "work," I have discovered that what is needed is an action that is totally unexpected, yet totally believable, and I have found that, for me, this is always an action which indicates that grace has been offered. And frequently it is an action in which the devil has been the unwilling instrument of grace. This is not a piece of knowledge that I consciously put into my stories; it is a discovery that I get out of them.

Sounds like life, like the many times people had a prearranged plan that came to a grinding halt, and they were forced to make a pivotal decision. You won't have to consciously place surprise in the story of anyone's life—including your own. Surprise is, as O'Connor put it, "a discovery." When you tell a story, take advantage of the element of surprise, and use it to inspire your listeners.

Finally, deliver the punch line boldly and clearly. Then *stop*. Don't explain the point ad infinitum (or ad nauseam!). State it once, state it clearly, and say it like you mean it. Then move on to the next thing on the agenda.

When you tell a story, take advantage of the element of surprise, and use it to inspire your listeners.

Be authentic in applying the lesson to your own life.
Obviously, if the story is about your experiences, it will be relatively easy to be genuine as you communicate the application. But always dig a little deeper to look for added meaning. Don't make something up just to sound profound, but ask the "why" and "what next" questions. Talk about the story with your spouse or a good friend. He or she may recall that the experience has shaped your life more deeply or in a different way than you remembered.

If the story is told in third person, make sure to connect the dots for people who are listening. Relate the lesson to your own life by saying, "This is what this story says to me," or, "Here's how I have applied [or will apply] the moral of this story." In any inspirational message, the "so what?" at the end is as essential as the details of the story. Don't rush past this crucial element! Take your time to craft your application statement so that the lights come on, heads nod, and people think: *I can do that too! In fact, I've got to do that!*

When you communicate the lesson and your application of it to your life, you open your heart a bit for others to see. That makes you real and approachable, but there's a risk too. It's not as risky as you might think, however. Some of you might say: *Oh, no. I've opened up and told everyone about my embarrassing mistake. Now they know I'm not 'all that'!* News flash: *They already knew it.* They just wanted to see if you would admit it.

If possible, use the story and the "so what?" application as a jumping-off point for discussion.
Your team, friends, or family will benefit from dialogue about the lesson of the story. In many cases, the story itself will bring up memories, desires, and goals—perhaps long buried but now resurrected. Ask open-ended questions that stimulate reflection and don't have simple answers: for instance, "Why do you think he did that?" or "How would you have

responded in the same situation?" And when people answer, don't jump in to challenge or correct them. Allow them to have different perspectives and arrive at dissimilar conclusions. Sometimes, people offer opposing views to see if you can be trusted. Don't overreact, and don't be defensive. Stay calm and ask them to tell you more of their perceptions.

Storytelling Is for All of Us

Some of us are natural storytellers, and we have the innate ability to weave a tale that captivates people. Depending on our personality type, we tend to choose stories that focus on particular subjects. For example:

- Commanders excel at telling stories about people who courageously faced seemingly insurmountable challenges and overcame incredible obstacles.

- Coaches enjoy talking about teams coming together to accomplish great things. Like Advocates, they are often quite at ease telling stories.

- Advocates often tell how someone faced a difficult problem and found a solution that changed thousands of lives.

- Accountability Partners like to share stories that explain how a single person's attention to detail made the difference between success and failure for a team or a company.

But no matter what our leadership style, *all* of us can learn to tell stories that inspire people, and with a little practice using the tips I just offered, we can only get better with time. Here's a case in point.

I once coached the CEO of a large New York corporation in how to uncover and communicate inspiring stories. Though this gentleman was very bright, he lacked the confidence to make inspiring presentations.

In our early conversations, I remember asking him a number of questions to find out what interested him. I soon learned that he is an avid pro football fan. He is especially enamored with legendary

Cowboys coach Tom Landry. This CEO had studied Landry's life and was impressed with his skill in selecting, motivating, and coaching his players. When he told me stories of Landry's leadership, his eyes lit up, and he became more animated than I had ever seen him. I recognized instantly his best source of inspiration.

Together, this CEO and I identified several noteworthy stories (like the tale of the famous "Ice Bowl" between Dallas and Green Bay) that he could include in his presentations to his top executives and stockholders. We discussed the lessons he learned from each story, and then crafted the wording so that he could speak eloquently about how those lessons shaped his own life. And it worked.

Now, all of that was already there, but this leader had just never put the pieces together before in a way that he could use to inspire others. Today when he speaks at such events, his past dread is replaced by genuine excitement. He is confident that he will connect with his audience—and he does.

FIND STORIES FROM HISTORY

Another deep source of stories is history. It's sad that a boring history teacher from the past has jaded so many people, but for those of us who were positively influenced, it is a never-ending source of inspiration. I'm looking over my shoulder at my bookshelves as I write this, and the inspiration factor rises as I scan the biographies of so many great people of the past. Each and every one of them had deep personal struggles and somehow found the strength not only to survive but also thrive in their circumstances.

I want to challenge you to give history another chance if you are inclined to dismiss the subject. If you are already a lover of history, consider becoming a champion of the stories and lessons of history. Here are some practical ways to use history as a source of inspiration.

1. Begin with a biography of a person you admire or are curious to learn more about. I would be the first to acknowledge that without

colorful people to focus on, history simply becomes a series of dates and events.

2. Then find the correlation between what was going on at that time in history and the times that we live in today. This is where it begins to get exciting because it now becomes relevant.

   Take the life and times of Abraham Lincoln, for example. The country was in turmoil; political parties were at each other's throats. The vision of one country, united under one flag, was at stake. Incredible injustice manifested in the form of slavery. Many Americans just wanted to stick their heads in the sand and ignore it.

   Just that background alone is enough for you to build an incredibly relevant and compelling story around.

3. After you have provided a relevant context, build out the main character—in this case, Lincoln. Just write a brief list from which to build a compelling story.

   • Grew up poor
   • Suffered fifteen major setbacks between 1831 and 1860, the year he was elected president
   • His closest staff member betrayed him more than once.

4. Now ask yourself, what are the potential lessons I can apply from this person's (Lincoln's) life that would make me a better leader? How can I use these "defining moments" in the person's (Lincoln's) life to inspire my team?

5. Finally, ask yourself, "What's the call to action from this story?" This is the payoff for making history come alive. Consider these few examples from a probable twenty or more such themes and calls to action:

   • Advance through your adversity.
   • Don't become a victim of your circumstances.
   • Don't allow betrayal to make you cynical.

To help you practice this approach, appendix C contains brief stories of four inspiring people—Winston Churchill, Mel Fisher, Queen

Elizabeth I, and Robert E. Lee—by outlining some of the life-changing events in their lives.

Any time you are in front of your team, company stockholders, your constituents, a class, your family, or anyone else you hope to inspire as you impart information, always—*always*—begin with a story. No matter what your personality type, you must master the art of telling stories if you are going to connect with people.

It's almost impossible to be boring when you are spinning a good yarn. On the other hand, it's impossible to *not* be boring when you're just sharing "the numbers," no matter how important they may be. People remember the mental images generated by our stories far better than they do facts, figures, and charts. The greatest communicator of all time, Jesus of Nazareth, could have overwhelmed people with his vast divine knowledge, but time after time, he told parables—*stories*—that captured people's hearts, communicated his message through narrative, and *inspired* them.

> People remember the mental images generated by our stories far better than they do facts, figures, and charts.

Think for a moment about the amazing success of a little periodical known as *Guideposts*. This publication is a hit precisely because of the inspirational *stories* found on every page. And one of the publishing marvels of recent decades is the Chicken Soup series, which is—what? Collections of stories that make us laugh, cry, and sigh.

Even in the high-pressure world of big business, top consultants are helping corporate executives realize the power of stories. Quoting Harvard psychologist Howard Gardner, in *Leading Minds*, "A key, perhaps the key, to leadership is . . . the effective communication of a story." Tom Peters expanded on Gardner's insight in *Leadership (Tom Peters Essentials)*, commenting: "Whether your gig involves primitive tribes or corporate tribes . . . the key to leadership is the (often unsung) Power of Storytelling. It was true in the bush. It's true in the boardroom. And it's true everywhere in between."

Let me close this chapter with an admonition: If you are inexperienced or unsure about your ability to tell inspiring stories, *develop* the skills you need in order to speak well. What do you hope to achieve in the lives of those who need inspiration? Put forth a little effort to find stories to that end, developing a deep reservoir of gripping narratives that you can craft for your team or family and make a difference in their lives. You *can* become a good storyteller. And if you are already a good one, you can become a *great* one.

Start today.

GET INSPIRED—TELL GREAT STORIES— YOURS AND OTHERS'

Outcome Objectives for Weeks Eight and Nine

- You will be able to develop and use a defining moment in your life to inspire someone else.
- You will be able to use a historical character or event to build an inspiring story around.
- You will be able to pull from many real-life experiences for the sake of building a portfolio of inspiring stories.

Equipping Yourself

1. What are your favorite movies? What do you like about them? Can you identify at least one life lesson you could apply from your favorite movie?
2. Who are the two or three best storytellers you know? How does their ability to craft and communicate great stories impact you?
3. Identify the most difficult moments or periods of your life.

- Are these your "defining moments"? Why or why not?
- What happened?
- How did they affect you at the time?
- What lessons did you learn then, or what lessons do you see now that you look back at those events?

4. What is one story from your own life that you enjoy telling? Why do you enjoy it?

5. Are there particular categories of events (such as sports, music, business, entertainment, or politics) that interest you? What are some stories in these categories that you enjoy hearing and telling?

6. Create a readily accessible file for stories you tear out of the newspaper, copy from online sources, or jot down on napkins. As you become more sophisticated in your research, you can create separate files for different categories.

7. On your weekly To Do sheet, add a regular item: "Craft a story that will inspire _____ (list the name of any person who especially needs a little inspiration)."

8. Review the tips in this chapter in the section titled "Craft Your Own Stories." Which of these do you do well? Which do you need to improve?

9. What is one thing you can do today or tomorrow to become a better storyteller?

Inspiring Others

1. Choose a team member or two and invite them to become an audience for you. Tell them to be as honest as possible as they listen to a story from you.

2. Take some time to finalize one story, and present it to your team or family this week. In your preparation:

   - Select a story that energizes you.
   - Identify the main points in the story and enough details to make it interesting.
   - Underline or memorize your first line.
   - Identify the lesson or "moral" you want to communicate from the story.
   - Craft an authentic "so what?" application of the lesson to your own life.

   After you tell the story, the lessons learned, and your own application, ask your listeners an open-ended question about how they would have responded in the same situation, or a similar question that elicits feedback.

3. Ask other members of your team to share stories with you and with the entire team. Praise them for the good points of their storytelling, and ask them if you can use their stories in your presentations.

GOING DEEPER

- Create a strategy for collecting customer/client stories that can be shared with your team, by your team.
- Create an internal contest to see who can write the most inspiring story. It can be tied to either a customer experience or a positive employee kind of experience. Use the contest as a way to stimulate the story-sharing principle.

Help People Reach Their Destination

What man actually needs is not a tensionless state but rather the striving and struggling for some goal worthy of him. What he needs is not the discharge of tension at any cost, but the call of a potential meaning waiting to be fulfilled by him.
—Viktor Frankl, Austrian neurologist, psychiatrist, Holocaust survivor

MY PERSONAL LIFE MISSION is to fan the embers of other people's potential into lives full of desire for a purpose bigger than themselves. I am absolutely, positively, crystal clear about this. It sure would have been helpful if I had been clear *before* changing majors three times in my undergraduate studies. But for most of us, it takes a while to get in touch with our internal GPS.

I believe that one way we can discern God's fingerprint on our beings is through our longing to know what direction our lives are to take in the world and for the world, while being responsible stewards of our talents and resources. It is an incredibly deep and powerful alignment when the two vectors merge.

But how can you inspire *others* to align their internal GPS with their destiny? It's hard to do if you have not done so for yourself. So, as part of the twelve-week challenge to create an inspiring culture, I want to help you accurately program your own internal GPS. As you try to determine your destination, you will probably notice certain signs along the way. Together, they will be the key to helping you understand whether or not you are headed toward your destination.

Programming Your Own Internal GPS

Notice I said *destination* and not *destiny*. Why? Because you do have a choice in deciding where you want to go with your life. In other words, you can get there *on purpose.*

As I alluded to earlier, my personal internal GPS has been set and reset many times. It was originally set toward becoming an inspirational speaker for high school students. Along the way I had some massive road-blocks to get through. The first time I made a public presentation, it was in Mandeville, Louisiana, at a Methodist Church camp. I thought it would be pretty safe. But about five minutes into my talk, a chaperone type came up onstage, shook my hand, and walked me offstage. I still cringe with embarrassment when I think about it. I felt like an *American Idol* reject. I very much wanted to alter the settings in my internal GPS to something a little safer, but the desire burned even deeper, so I stayed the course.

Another time I was tempted to alter the settings was when I actually started trying to support a family of five. It was, at times, just plain scary. All of you who have started a business or lived on commission know the feeling. The voices around me got louder and louder: "What's wrong with getting a regular job? Do you think you are too good for that?" The good news is that my internal GPS led me to a destination that made it possible to speak face-to-face to more than 500,000 high school students during that period of time. To this day, thanks to Facebook, I still hear from former students—some of whom are parents now—about the impact many of those encounters had on them.

Most of the time when we alter the settings of our internal GPS, it is not by our own choice. To put it another way, we don't usually get up in the morning and say out loud, "Gee, Wally/Sally, I think I will start doing something different today." Are you nodding in agreement and understanding? No, we typically consider changing our destinations on the other side of a life-altering event.

RESETTING YOUR GPS

What recent event has occurred in your life that is causing you to adjust your internal GPS settings? Recently, three of my clients from around the country were told that they were being laid off. There's no telling how many of you reading this will receive similar, life-altering news in the near future, if you haven't already. Whether its health, divorce, or career related, it will be something you did not sign up for, and you will want to opt out. During these times you will be forced to reconsider your destination— and you will want to make adjustments to your internal GPS.

Such an event occurred in my life when my brother Ken, just eighteen months my elder, was diagnosed with colon cancer, and six months later, died from complications of chemotherapy. The loss of my brother was immensely painful, as any of you who have experienced the same will know. Afterward, garnering the strength and extreme energy it took to speak to five thousand high school students at a time was more than I could physically or emotionally do. I needed to find a destination that would allow me to grieve and heal—yet use the gifts of a communicator all the while.

That's how direction is determined for most of us, is it not? We search for a new environment that provides us with four crucial factors:

1. It is a place in which we feel challenged.
2. It gives us an opportunity we can retool our skills to exploit.
3. It is aligned with our life mission.
4. It allows us to be paid according to our value.

So, I dialed my internal GPS toward a values-oriented entertainment company to produce animated stories about such American heroes as Thomas Edison, William Bradford, Benjamin Franklin, and others. Taking what I had learned about high school assembly programs, I began to recruit professional actors who dressed like the animated characters in the stories. Then I wrote inspirational scripts for large audiences, and educated tens of thousands of people across America. In the end, these folks also bought a lot of animated stories for their children.

With many, if not most, changes in direction, there is someone who mysteriously merges into your lane and connects with you. For the next setting of my internal GPS, this "chance" meeting took place during lunch at a Chili's restaurant in Houston.

I had made friends through my speaking with a media consultant named Duncan Dodds, who is now chief of staff for the iconic minister Joel Osteen. At that lunch, Duncan had brought a friend who was in the launching stage of a new venture that involved reaching the youth market. In the course of casual conversation, I listened carefully to the vision of this entrepreneur. I was moved by his passion and determination to reach his destination. He was clearly following his own internal GPS.

Without hesitation, I began to share what I had learned about effectively reaching youth. An hour later, we shook hands, exchanged cards, and said our good-byes.

As soon as the man's Honda had left the Chili's parking lot, Duncan, who stands six feet, eight inches tall, grabbed me by the shoulder, looked down into my eyes, and said with the stern voice of a principal, "Barber, the next time I hear you giving away that kind of valuable information for free, I'm going to kick your butt." I was stunned. He went on, "People will pay you money for what you just gave away."

That day Duncan challenged me: the next time someone dared ask for my advice, I was to dare ask for a check. I had no idea what that really meant at the time, but I promised I would use the script he carefully wrote out for me on a page in my Day-Timer: "I am happy to share with you what I have learned through the years about reaching your audience. Would you like to set up a time to visit face-to-face? My fee is $500.00 for a half day." I must have read it a hundred times over the next three days.

Then the follow-up call came from Duncan's lunch companion. "I really enjoyed our time together the other day," he said. "I'd like to get together again and pick your brain some more." Instantly, I pulled out the Day-Timer page Duncan had written on, and I read it verbatim. "I am happy to share . . ."

"I don't have a problem with that," he said when I'd finished my three-sentence speech. "Please send your invoice in advance."

I quickly dialed into my internal GPS the destination "consultancy," and for the next fifteen years, I purposely followed that signal one way or another.

Who is the Duncan in your life? What is he or she saying to you? It is the people who know you best who can guide you most.

The last adjustment I made to my internal GPS was simply the result of trying to clearly define for myself my personal USP (unique selling proposition). I began to ask some of the most influential people in my life—who are also strong leaders—"If you had to name the most critical driving force behind your choosing the destination you chose, what would it be?" Surprisingly, their responses had little to do with their ambition for a specific role or title. I never heard one person say, "I want to be the boss."

What I did hear, over and over again, was strikingly similar to what Oprah said concerning what inspired her to success, and what my wife, Debbi, recalls about what made her choose to "make something of herself" (see Principle 3—See in Others the Abilities They Don't See in Themselves). It was not a desire for some*thing* that inspired them. It was some*one*. Likewise, for these leaders, the driving force that altered their destinations and inspired them to greatness was *someone* speaking a word of encouragement into their lives at the right time.

I once again reset my destination. This time I set my internal GPS toward living and working on Inspiration Blvd., a place where people from around the world could come and be inspired and, in turn, inspire others. If you have not yet visited inspirationblvd.com, you owe it to yourself to do so. The vision was to create an online community where people could make their life stories meaningful to others. Today, on inspirationblvd. com, there are inspiring stories for every occasion, whether it's for a team meeting or corporate training. Perhaps a story of personal triumph is more what you need for the day. But the driving motivation of all who post their stories is the hope that what they have learned and what they share will be inspiring to someone else at the right time.

I also wanted to create a way to honor the inspirational heroes of our lives, and that's what I have achieved. On inspirationblvd.com, you can upload a photo of someone who inspired you, write something about what he or she said or did that moved you, publish your story, and even forward it to that person or other friends. Day in and day out, I help people and organizations create inspiring environments, one inspirational transaction at a time.

So, what is your unique selling proposition—your USP? What's the one thing you do better than anyone else around you? What kind of resident specialist can you become right where you are? If by chance you are looking for your unique place and role, this is probably a really good time to consider a new destination.

Following the Road Signs

I mentioned at the beginning of my story that there will be signs along the way to help you know whether or not you are headed in the right direction. Here are just a few well-known, easily read signs.

WARNING: WRONG DIRECTION

"I hate Monday mornings with a purple passion." Guess what? That's a really bad sign that you just might be headed in the wrong direction and need to spend some time getting in touch with your internal GPS. On every journey, we will always find a few unpleasant things about getting there. Maybe road food is really unappealing, or you are consistently stuck in the middle seat of an airplane, in the back, next to the toilet. I can think of a hundred things as a traveler that I don't like about the journey. But I stay dialed in because I know from the inside out that I am headed in the right direction.

But if I ever get to a point where I am saying week in and week out, "This is no fun anymore," I will have to stop and evaluate whether I am still going in the right direction. Just last week, I heard these very words from an individual who attended one of our seminars. She is not unlike many I have met. She started in her job as just a way to feed her family. Not a bad motivation, I might add. But rather than honing her GPS during this small detour, she got sucked into the corporate vacuum. Does she have the proper skills for what she does? You bet. Is she appreciated? Yes. But is it getting her any closer to the destination that is coming from within her heart? No. "Every night when I lie down," she told me, "I just think, *How much longer can I keep doing this?*"

What came to mind as I listened to her story was that annoying voice blaring at me from within the Hertz NeverLost navigation system: "Make a legal U-turn when possible." This lady needed to make a U-turn and listen to her internal GPS. But is it not true that the farther down the road you get, the more difficult it is to turn around? "I've come this far," we say. "Let me just see where this will take me." Or, "It's so far back, I don't have enough gas or money to get all the way there."

If this is you, let me encourage you to pull off to the side of the road you are on, make a U-turn, and start following the internal GPS that you programmed a long time ago. Perhaps it's simply a decision to consider changing direction. That's okay. It's a good place to start.

WARNING: NO ENTHUSIASM AHEAD!

Inspiration is the spark that ignites your ability to see what is possible. Enthusiasm is the fuel you will need to take the actions that will make what is possible a reality. I can promise you this: if you have no genuine enthusiasm for your destination, you will run out of the emotional and physical fuel needed to complete the trip. And it's something that can't be faked—for long, anyway.

I have a friend with whom I golf on a fairly regular basis. Much of our conversation typically revolves around his dream to somehow be plugged into world missions one day. It's not that he hates Mondays or even dislikes the people he works with. To quote him exactly, "I just don't have a lot of passion about what I do." Unfortunately, his lack of enthusiasm shows up in his absenteeism, his fatigue, and his overall demeanor.

If this sounds like you, consider turning the volume up on your internal GPS and heading toward a destination that you can be enthusiastic about. It really does not have to be anything as noble as world missions. And it does not even have to be your job in its entirety. It can be some aspect of your work that energizes you, or someone in whom you have taken a special interest in hopes of inspiring that person to greatness. Nothing gives birth to enthusiasm better than helping others take the next step in reaching their goals.

My friend and colleague Gary Jones is the chief human resource officer at Grizzard Communications Group. He and his team are the front line for all employee issues; they hear them all the time. If there is anyone who should have a reason to look like they just lost their best friend, it's the people in HR. Yet, when I walk into Gary's office and ask, "So, how is it going?" he enthusiastically responds: "I have to tell you, I love what I'm doing here. Let me show you what I'm working on that I think will help improve our culture here even more . . ."

People like Gary are incredibly attractive and inspiring because they are so enthused about what they do. That's not to say that he loves everything he has to do, because there is nothing enjoyable about certain aspects of his job. But he sees the bigger picture of what he does, how he is making a difference in our company's culture, and how he can help more people actually have fun doing their work.

Another person who comes to mind when I think of enthusiasm for one's work is my friend Michelle Tafoya at the University of California–Davis. Michelle has a passionate, visible hunger for knowledge and coaching. When we are together, she wants to move swiftly through benchmarking and projection-type activities so she can spend our remaining time together just asking questions: "How can I be a better manager?" "What would make me more valuable in my role?" "How can I extend my sphere of influence?"

Enthusiasm is not a personality trait. It will transcend all four of the personality types—Commander, Coach, Advocate, and Accountability Partner—*if* you're headed toward the right destination.

WARNING: GOING IN CIRCLES

Another road sign that will help you know if you are headed in the right direction is much subtler than the previous signs. See if this sounds familiar. You are following your internal GPS, but for whatever the reason, you begin to see sights and signs that look way too familiar. You blow it off as just a coincidence. But at some point you realize you are no closer to your destination now than you were when you first embarked on the journey. Debbi and I literally experienced this when we were driving to a wedding in Madison, Wisconsin, and passed one particular farmhouse three times! It was frustrating for us not to be making any progress toward our destination, and it can be frustrating for you as well.

Many times we cannot seem to get any closer to our destination, though we are clear about what it is, because we continually sabotage ourselves through a pattern of poor decisions and choices. For example, I have a client who I personally enjoy working with, but evidently, her team does not. She has just hired her fifth marketing manager in the last three years. She is also on her third assistant in the same period of time, and other direct reports move in and out of her shop as if through a revolving door. One day over lunch, she was lamenting about how difficult it was to find good hires these days, and how she longed to find people who would work as hard as she does. I took a chance and asked the hard question: "So, what is the one common denominator with every hire you have been unhappy with?"

I don't know if she just could not see it or did not have the courage to say it, but it was pretty clear to everyone else: *she* was the common denominator. It was hard for me to tell her the truth, but I knew she was going to continue to make big, looping circles over and over again until she made an internal adjustment regarding her character and the way she worked with other people.

I have three exhortations for those of you who may have your GPS set right but continue to find yourselves passing that same John Deere tractor: (1) be open to correction; (2) take responsibility for making the circle; and (3) realize that if you don't change from the inside out, you will keep coming back to this same place over and over again.

WARNING: LOTS OF MONEY AHEAD!

At first glance, this sign would appear to affirm the direction in which you are headed. But by the looks of the carnage on the side of the road, many have apparently traveled this road before and not made it to their destination. Others continued on, made it, and picked up their money, but in the process, they had to leave more valuable things behind.

When we hear people who have amassed so much wealth say, "Hey, it's not all it's cracked up to be," it's natural for those of us on a lower financial plane to respond, "Easy for you to say." But if you don't believe these words are true, listen to legendary automaker Lee Iacocca, who lamented, "Here I am in the twilight years of my life, still wondering what it's all about; I can tell you this: fame and fortune is for the birds"; or Walker Percy, the Southern "philosophical novelist," who said, "You can get all As and still flunk life."

The point is, when you are pursuing your destination, please consider factoring in something that gives meaning to your life beyond just money. William James observed, "The greatest use of a life is to spend it for something that outlasts it." I couldn't agree more. For one's life to be truly significant, a person has to find something bigger than himself to factor into his destination of choice, a cause that he's convinced will make a difference in the world.

While speaking to a group of professional fund-raisers in New Orleans this past year, one man in particular caught my attention. His name is Robert, and he serves as the chief operating officer for a nonprofit corporation whose mission is the prevention of child abuse through parenting classes, anger-management counseling, and mentoring. Before this, he was the COO of the largest real estate title company in America. I have known many great executives who have had to refocus because of the economic downturn, layoffs, and permanent downsizings. Some have redirected their lives and talent toward the nonprofit world. Robert, on the other hand, changed directions voluntarily—simply because he wanted to make a difference in the world.

And he is not alone. Bob Buford of Halftime has garnered literally thousands of wildly successful business executives who are now using their skills in the nonprofit sector in hopes of making a difference. (For more information about this inspirational community, see www.halftime.org.)

My point? We all need to make a living, and obviously, the more money you have, the more you can do. But if money is all that drives you, at some point your destination will seem very unfulfilling. At the end of the day, you, like Mr. Iacocca, will be wondering what it's all about.

Sometimes when I am in a new location, and I don't know exactly where I am going, I plug "city-center" into my GPS. At least I know I'll be going in the right direction while I figure out my specific route. This is exactly how you can help someone begin to figure out her potential points of destination. Get that individual headed in the right direction and let her figure out a specific destination for herself.

Let's get started. We will first focus on making sure your internal GPS is properly set and then turn our attention toward helping your team members program their own internal GPS.

GET INSPIRED—HELP PEOPLE REACH THEIR DESTINATION

Outcome Objectives for Weeks Ten and Eleven

- You will be able to be specific about your point(s) of destination regarding your reputation and your career.
- You will be able to help your team set their internal GPS according to their dreams and your corporate objectives.

Equipping Yourself

For these activities, you will need to develop three surveys. You will complete the first one; a coworker who knows you well will complete the second; and your best client or customer will complete the third. By comparing your responses with those of your colleague and your customer/client, you should get a well-rounded and honest perspective about where you are presently headed.

1. On the survey you develop for yourself, record the following:

    -   A minimum of five adjectives that accurately describe you

    -   Three work-related activities that energize you

    -   The one thing you think your client, customer, or boss values most about you

    -   The one thing you will always want for your life, no matter what your job, your pay, or your circumstances

2. Give the following assessment to both a coworker who knows you well and to your best client or customer. Ask them to answer the questions honestly as they apply to you:

    -   What five adjectives (more if you can think of them) best describe me?

    -   What three work-related activities do you believe are the most energizing to me?

    -   What one thing do you value most about me?

    -   What, in your opinion, is the one thing I will always want for my life, no matter what my job, pay, or circumstances?

3. Next, you will rename your job title to reflect your impact, not your role. Use the three completed surveys to help you in this task.

    I confess, in the early days of doing this with our team, it made the HR folks crazy: we were trying to make up strange-sounding titles to print on business cards. But afterward, I made it a point to get everybody some cards bearing their new titles, even if they never had occasion to give them out. It's amazing how much ROI (return on investment) I got out of those twelve-dollar boxes of business cards.

    One title that came out of this exercise was "Team Enforcer: I Make Things Go." I loved that one! Another was "Implementer: I Am the Bridge between Strategy and Execution." We also created one that quickly spread to other teams: "Strategist: Connecting the Dots of Information to Get Results." And then there was the title they bestowed on me, which I fell in love with and use even now: Chief Inspirator. (It doesn't even need a tagline.)

Declaring your title is both visionary and prophetic. What's more, it will render you closer to discovering the address you need to key into your internal GPS.

4. Finally, you will help your team one by one create a new kind of résumé. Do this for yourself first, and then lead your team through this activity.

At the top of the page, under your name, write your newfound title. On the occupational objective line, where you usually put things like "Looking for ways to use my great strengths as a _____," you will write your life mission statement behind the following words: "Looking for anything to do that will allow me to _____."

Under the category of experience, don't bother to list past employment. Instead, make a list of all the jobs you want to have before you retire.

Again, you are uncovering nothing about a past that, frankly, most of us overvalue anyway. You are instead helping to dial in a number of potential points of destination. The really fun part is that if you are taking a team through this as a supervisor type, you just crystallized much of your own new job description: to help your team members reach at least one of their points of destination.

Even as you begin to visualize this happening in your mind's eye, you have got to be sensing the inspiration factor climbing.

5. Create your résumé by following the steps below:

   (a) Under your name, place your *new* title.

   (b) Beneath this, add the words "Looking for anything to do that will allow me to." Now, based on what makes you tick, complete the sentence.

   (c) Where you would typically place your "past experience," list all of the positions you would like to hold before you retire. Be honest about your desires. The sky's the limit!

Inspiring Others

1. Have each member of your team create a page with two columns. On the left have them list eight to ten people they hope have high opinions of them. Encourage them to include clients/customers, supervisors, colleagues, and direct reports. On the right, have them write eight to ten words that they would like for the people they listed on the left to use when describing them. Tell them that these words are to be *points of destination* for their individual reputations.

Then, as they think about the words they listed, ask them to determine what types of actions they will need to take to move in that direction. Discuss their conclusions.

2. Review with your teammates the four warning signs mentioned in this chapter. Then lead the members of your team in a discussion about their own experiences with these warning signs. What other signs can your team mention that might indicate they are headed in the wrong direction?

3. Lead your team in a discussion about how the intersection of skills, past experience, and market need came together for them. (Or *has* it come together for them?)

4. One way to help someone set his internal GPS is to get him pointed toward a "city-center" of life. Have each of your team members complete the Equipping Yourself exercises for this chapter, as you did.

   - As they prepare their résumés, under the heading "Career Objective," ask them to write the kind of impact they want to have within the organization.

   - Under the category of experience, again ask them to think in terms of the future, not the past. This time, though, rather than listing titles that they would like to hold, have them write down their most desired job *functions* for their next two to three career moves. In other words, what do they want to be *doing* for the next few years of their lives?

5. Spend some time at your next team meeting allowing team members to introduce each other based on what they have learned regarding the direction of their teammates. For example: "To my right is Susan, who presently serves as The Implementer on our team. Her greatest strength is that she makes things 'go' for us. Her plans for the future include (doing the same but even better) or (contributing more in creative services), etc."

   Beginning with yourself, introduce the person to your right. That person will then introduce the individual to his or her right, and so on, until everyone has been introduced.

   Consider inviting another team to this session to model and inspire others in the organization.

GOING DEEPER

Create a road map that illustrates where you have been in your career and where your point(s) of destination are in the future. Consider even listing what the milestones along the path will be.

Create a New Culture

There can be no transforming of darkness into light and
of apathy into movement without emotion.
—Carl Jung, Swiss psychiatrist, author

BEFORE HE COACHED UCLA, there had never been anyone like him. There probably never will be again.

College basketball junkies know that John Wooden's Bruins won ten national titles, including an unprecedented seven in a row from 1967 to 1973. Impressive, yes, but his players know something even better than that. They know that John Wooden is far more than just a great coach; he is also a brilliant teacher, a caring mentor, and a source of *inspiration*. In fact, according to former UCLA All-Star Bill Walton, Coach Wooden surpasses all of UCLA's great sports heroes, from Jackie Robinson to Kareem Abdul-Jabbar, in impact. In a tribute titled "John Wooden, Like UCLA, Simply the Best," Walton wrote of the coach that "What he has is a heart, brain, and soul that put him in a position to inspire others to reach levels of success and peace of mind that we could never dream of reaching by ourselves." (Available at www.billwalton.com/wooden.html.)

Wooden's coaching style was understated and low-key. He never yelled or screamed at his players, and he never ranted at the officials. He also never asked his players to do anything that he wasn't already doing. And though every coach wants his team to *win*, Wooden's players never heard him utter the word. In fact, while many coaches were busy creating a high-pressure culture of rivalry, hostility, obsession, and success at any cost, Wooden was focusing simply on imparting character and teaching the fundamentals of the game. Walton went on to write that Wooden taught his players "how to build a foundation based on . . . human values and personal characteristics" that enabled them to perform at their peak whenever the moment demanded it.

Coach Wooden created an environment in which players wanted to learn everything he could teach them. He made them thirsty to be the best they could be. In a phrase, he *built a new culture*.

No one would deny that Wooden, now quite elderly, was successful. His success as a coach speaks for itself. But his success as teacher and mentor is shown in the affection and admiration of those who played for him. He created perhaps the most powerfully positive culture of inspiration in the history of sports, and his players will never forget it.

Cultivating DNA

Inspiring someone once is good, but it's only a start. For our affirmation to take root and have real impact, we have to be consistent, tenacious, and creative. These attributes have to become part of our organization's and our household's DNA, that is, their *culture*. Only then will employees, team members, spouses, and children believe that we really mean what we say about their dreams and their abilities to reach them.

To create a corporate culture of inspiration, we, as leaders, first have to analyze our roles. Our task is to blend three things: *outcomes, people,* and *processes*.

- Our *outcomes* are defined by company shareholders, executives above us, or perhaps by us. These are the external measurements of success consisting of production, share price, profits, and market share.

- Our conception of *people* can range from seeing them as cogs in our machine to talented partners with whom we work honestly and openly.

- Our perception of the organization's goals will determine the *processes* we use to organize people to accomplish those goals.

Each of us can see our role the way John Wooden envisioned his: as teachers committed to excellence and character development. Wooden wasn't just a cheerleader uttering empty slogans. As much as any leader, he valued outcomes, but he never used people to accomplish self-centered goals. The development of individuals was every bit as important as winning basketball games. We need to follow his example, making both the place where we work and the place where we live a culture of *personal development*. Just as Coach Wooden saw basketball as a way of preparing his players for the ultimate game of life, we need to help our team see that our work is important, but it is not life itself.

In other words, our work should be a training ground for developing our skills, using our talents, and building our long-term value. In that way, we will have a team that performs well for customers/clients, bosses, and stockholders. This approach to work is not just about being happy. It's about performance that yields superior results.

We need to follow college basketball coach John Wooden's example, making both the place where we work and the place where we live a culture of *personal development*.

BUILDING A CULTURE OF INSPIRATION: BEWARE THE BUSTERS

As you probably already know by comparing people's varied reactions to the same event, some folks thrive when the unexpected takes place; they simply improvise. But too much routine can squelch their personalities and stunt their inspiration. On the other hand, some people can't survive *without* a rigid, unchanging daily structure. When taken by surprise, they are crippled, and all inspiration is lost.

In our role as teacher and coach of our employees (and children), we need to carefully observe the things that kill their inspiration. If we study the different profiles in the personality inventory in this book (or any other), we'll have a good idea both of what inspires people and of what saps their enthusiasm.

Here's a synopsis of inspiration busters for each of the four personality types I've described in this book:

> Commanders thrive on challenges, but they chafe when the goals are muddy, they get mixed messages from their leaders, or if others' expectations of them are too low. If you want to de-inspire a Commander, just try telling him he's not big enough for the "stage" when his heart was already set on being the "leading man."

> Coaches enjoy pulling a team together to accomplish tasks, but once the mission is accomplished, their enthusiasm will be crushed if the only ones thanked for a job well done are the team members. Obviously, the team deserves to be appreciated for their efforts, but if you fail to acknowledge a Coach's contributions as well, then you have successfully put her inspiration to death. (*Note:* Coaches also suffer de-inspiration under rigid rules, lack of variety in assignments, or isolation from the group.)

> Advocates wilt under harsh criticism. They also don't do well under pressure to "hurry up and get 'er done." To keep an Advocate inspired, you'd better give him time to be creative—and then affirm him lavishly for his efforts. If he feels for even a moment that his contribution is not valued, his inspiration will drain as through a sieve.

Accountability Partners, like Advocates, hate being rushed. Worse, they despise chaos, because Accountability Partners are *committed to excellence*. If you want to squash the inspiration of an Accountability Partner, then maintain a chaotic environment in which confusion rules and expectations are loosely defined. But if you want to inspire her to greatness, make sure that hers is an *ordered* environment where she is free to focus on systems, without distraction, and where attention to detail—especially hers—is valued.

In case you can't tell by now, I'm a Coach. I love working with people and getting to know them so I can tailor my leadership to challenge them, affirm them, and provide structure or variety for them according to their specific need. I enjoy being thrown into complex situations where I have to sort out people's goals and their relationships with each other. When I'm able to help them overcome roadblocks that have hindered them from being successful, I feel like a million dollars! But on those occasions when I feel alone and I have to follow a set of arbitrary and unnecessary rules, I become discouraged. My creativity evaporates, and my energy level dissipates. It's not a pretty sight.

Everybody on your team or in your family will eventually come in contact with an inspiration killer. It's unavoidable. We can, however, be good students of those we lead so that we avoid crushing their spirits. Sometimes, rules must be followed, people have to work alone, work is boring, and change upsets the status quo. But good leaders have built a culture of concern and trust. They have watched, listened, and identified the individual needs of their team—and their team members know it. So, even when inspiration tilts a little toward the downside, it doesn't take long to get everyone back on track.

But how *does* a leader build such a culture, one in which *every* member can be inspired to personal excellence?

Everybody on your team or in your family will eventually come in contact with an inspiration killer. It's unavoidable. We can, however, be good students of those we lead so that we avoid crushing their spirits.

BUILDING A CULTURE OF INSPIRATION: BE INTENTIONAL

Creating an inspiring culture doesn't just happen; it requires planning, discipline, and practice. The very first step in the process, however, is a ruthless commitment to *objectivity*. Some of us have tolerated the use of caustic words, attitudes, body language, and overtly negative actions so long that these destructive influences have become our DNA. They now spill out not only of us but also of those who follow our example.

Or perhaps we dole out mixed messages: sometimes ones of appreciation, at other times (often more frequently), ones of condemnation. We feel *so* good about the praise we give, but we discount the impact of the poison we sometimes excrete. Actually, psychologists tell us that mixed messages are even more powerfully manipulative than consistently negative ones, because mixed messages produce a toxic blend of hope and fear in others: the hope that they'll be praised and the fear that they'll be ridiculed or ignored.

It's not sufficient, however, to simply stop giving negative messages. Nature, as the physicists say, abhors a vacuum, and such is the case with negative messages. They must be *replaced* with kindness, affirmation, vision, and hope. Even when people fail, our correction can inspire instead of destroy. Subtle shifts in the tone of our voice, in our conversation, can have dramatic results. We can say: "I'm confident this isn't your best work [or the kind of attitude you want to have]. I believe in you, and I know you can do better. I'll help any way that I can."

Our words, though, aren't the only means by which we communicate with one another. Actually, words make up only 7 percent of communication. The impact of our facial expressions and body language is even more important. We need to be aware of the look in our eyes as well as the words that come out of our mouths.

The 360 Profile is a valuable tool to use to find out what kind of messages you communicate to the people around you. Let me encourage you to take the feedback with grace and humility. You may not like it, but don't disregard it. Instead, ask people to tell you more about their perceptions. Change can be difficult, but the best leaders know they have to make adjustments to be at their best and to create a culture in which others are at their best.

To go about making changes, break them down into bite-size chunks with manageable, measurable action steps. People who feel they have to change everything at once usually change nothing. Isolate the points of change (and we all can improve, even the best leaders among us), and prioritize them. Ask for assistance from a mentor, coach, or supervisor, and jump in with both feet. If it feels awkward at first, don't be alarmed. We felt awkward when we first learned to ride bikes as kids, but soon it became second nature. In the same way, new perceptions and skills will become second nature—part of the fabric of our DNA—as we practice them.

To radically change the culture and climate in your office and home, let me offer a few broad suggestions as well as the specifics of weekly and monthly planning.

Know your people.
Take some time to think about each person on your team, jot down the "inspiration busters" for each, and then identify the things you do and say that might kill his or her motivation. Also, list the person's strengths and needs according to the profile's description, and keep that information close at hand for the next month to remind you what to expect from each person and to tailor your communication to each in order to be most effective. After a month, this information should be ingrained in your mind. It will shape your interactions with people.

Prepare!

Before each team meeting, do your homework. Find an appropriate story—your own or someone else's—that will inspire your team. (Review Principle 5—Tell Great Stories: Yours and Others'—for preparation tips.) Then practice it, making sure you have a fitting conclusion that connects the dots for your listeners so that the story's lesson will be clear. Also consider the agenda for the meeting, and determine how you can best blend the organization's desired outcomes, the people involved, and the process for directing them in order to inspire them to excellence.

Notice, name, and nurture.

We talked about this at length in Principle 2 (Connect with Others' Dreams), but it bears repeating.

Whether in the conference room or in your kitchen, as you get to know each person better, you'll find out what makes him or her tick. Notice each person's dreams and abilities, name them, and nurture them. You'll be amazed at how much it means to people when you take an extra minute or two to affirm them. It will transform the entire culture. Every person under your leadership will be more animated, more disciplined, and more effectual.

Build a team spirit.

Let's face it: Some people are extremely high-control leaders, and they expect people to jump when they say a single word. A few of them are powerful enough to actually command that kind of respect, but in the vast majority of cases when I've seen this demand in action, the leaders are just megalomaniacs who thrive on dominating others.

Then there are others who are not so overt but can nevertheless still threaten (much like my dad did trying to motivate me by threatening punishment if I did not start getting better grades). It is easy for managers and supervisors to play this role: "Do it like I want or else you'll be fired." "Be loyal and supportive of me or else you'll never get promoted."

But the more we feel comfortable in our own skins—authentic about our strengths and our weaknesses—the better able we will be to lower the demands and invite people to participate on a genuine team. Instead of mandating compliance, we will ask others to share their opinions, with this outcome: we won't become defensive if they disagree with us. I love to see secure leaders respond to a team member who brings up a different point of view by saying: "That's an interesting position. Tell me more about what you're thinking."

In that environment, every person on the team feels included, energized, accepted, and inspired to do his or her best work. Best of all, the whole team will be more accepting of the varied views of its members. They will work better together—all because you have successfully fostered a team spirit.

Changing the Culture—It's a Process

We love dramatic stories—think of Indiana Jones, the Bourne trilogy, *Mission Impossible*, and anything featuring Bruce Willis. On a few occasions, as leaders have sought to build an inspiring culture, their stories were equally dramatic. I've personally witnessed such *extraordinary* change.

The Bible contains some of the most dramatic moments in all of literature, such as the parting of the Red Sea, or the little shepherd boy David killing the Philistine giant Goliath with a stone from a sling. But more often than not, change happens more slowly. When Jesus taught people about change, he often used agrarian metaphors. A farmer's tilling of the soil and planting of the seed, plus a *season* of warmth and rain, result in the harvest. It doesn't magically appear, and it doesn't come instantly. The process of nurturing the plant to fruition takes time and work, but eventually, diligent farmers are rewarded with a good harvest.

In my work of helping to change the culture of teams, divisions, companies, and families, I've found that most supervisors and spouses are thrilled with the efforts of those who diligently seek to build an inspiring culture. In fact, they've been hoping for these changes for a long time! But in a few isolated instances, supervisors have resisted these changes and belittled managers for taking steps to build a team spirit. When that happens, I encourage these managers to keep inspiring their teams, but not to advertise it too broadly. Usually, the positive benefits the team experiences will eventually cause reluctant supervisors to admit that inspiring people is worth it after all.

If insecure supervisors still condemn managers who are trying to motivate their teams, I encourage these managers to look for another place to serve. In the meantime, however, they are to continue to be a positive force for inspiration where they are. There's something powerful about being faithful to the principles of inspiration despite your boss or your environment as a whole. Sooner or later, someone who matters is bound to notice. And worst case, even if no one notices, you can feel good about not allowing someone else to steal your sense of well-being, because its not theirs to take. Remember, it is your internal peace. No one can take it from you. You alone would have to give it up.

On our teams, we can expect a range of responses to our efforts to change the culture. Various studies, including that conducted by Everett M. Rogers, who documented it in his book, *Diffusion of Innovations*, identify reactions ranging from "early adopters" who internalize concepts quickly and become supportive of change almost from the outset, to "middle adopters," "late adopters," and those who resist change at all costs. We really appreciate team members who nod when we're introducing new material and can't wait to implement it, but we shouldn't see these eager folks as the norm.

Most people take the "I'm from Missouri. Show me" approach, and they require their leaders to prove the value of the change before they get on board. A few hear the concept, see it modeled, and watch as the rest of the team implements the changes, but they refuse to budge until they are sure all the bugs have been worked out and there's no chance for failure. Thankfully, not many people in the workforce are late adopters, and at the far end of the spectrum, those who resist to the death don't last long in most companies!

ORGANIZATIONAL CULTURES CAN CHANGE

You *can change* your culture, one principle at a time, one inspirational transaction at a time. No matter where you are in the organization, you can be a lightning rod for inspiration.

You *can change* your culture, one principle at a time, one inspirational transaction at a time. No matter where you are in the organization, you can be a lightning rod for inspiration.

Develop a weekly plan.

Some of us just let our weekly team meetings happen. We do minimal planning, except to print out sales reports or something else we need to cover. But to create a culture of inspiration, we have to do better than that. We need to take a few minutes to craft a plan so that people leave team meetings thinking, *Man, that was fantastic! I can't wait to get to work,* instead of *Good grief. That was a waste of time.*

In your plan, consider these elements:

> **The Attention Grabber.** Begin your meeting with an arresting story about someone who did something courageous and noble. These kinds of stories can be the basis for developing a collection of corporate parables (stories with a meaning). You can find examples on inspirationblvd.com.

> **"Show and Tell."** Ask different people to communicate one of their defining moments to the team. (These often take a while to share and digest because they tap into people's emotions, so you may want to save this activity for longer, monthly meetings. Still, the weekly meeting may be a good time to preselect the next person to share his or her defining moment. This will give the individual time to think about ways to tell the story in a manner that will inspire the whole team. This is also a great opportunity to invite senior leadership in to share specific defining moments in the development and growth of the company.)

> These defining moments can be events from the distant past or simply everyday events that happen at work, both positive *and* negative. Encourage your team to be honest. Team members suffer if we create a climate that tells them they're in big trouble if they

have dissatisfied clients. But if we promote the idea that difficult moments become life-changing lessons, team members won't lie to each other or try to hide their struggles. When your people feel free to communicate their struggles and the lessons they learned in dealing with management or customers, *everybody* on the team benefits.

The Rose-Pinning Ceremony. This activity comes in two parts. First, point out the strengths and contributions of at least one team member, maybe more, and be sure you share these affirmations equally as the weeks go by, so that in time, every team member feels noticed and all of their strengths are named and nurtured.

The second part of this activity involves the *entire* team. Share the team's successes since the last meeting. My wife, Debbi, often tells stories about satisfied clients, full of specifics and quotes to highlight the contribution of each team member.

Something that I've implemented in team meetings is to ask members to identify strengths in the teammate to their right. In this way, inspiration doesn't just come from me. Over the years, I've watched these lateral affirmations create very strong ties, smooth communications, and build a culture of loyalty. This is one of the most effective team-building activities I know.

I've watched lateral affirmations, in which members identify strengths in the teammate to their right, create very strong ties, smooth communications, and build a culture of loyalty.

All of these elements of a team meeting aren't just fluff, and they aren't wasted time. They provide opportunities for members of the team to build bridges of understanding, and they provide insights about people and the work to be done so that adjustments can be made in plans for the future. For example, as I get to know people's passions, I assign responsibilities more effectively, and I tailor the work to fit each person's abilities.

These seemingly minor alterations result in greater efficiency, higher productivity, fewer conflicts and misunderstandings, and more satisfied customers. That's not a bad outcome.

As time goes by, your people will look forward to these team meetings because they're convinced that these times together will be meaningful. A few minutes of preparation promises to produce inspiration and deeper connections among team members. Yes, it takes some time to prepare, and yes, it takes time to share these thoughts in the meeting. The question you have to ask is, "Is it worth it?" My answer, after watching the light come on in people's eyes over and over again, is, "You bet it is!"

Create inspirational transactions.
Do not be 100 percent reliant on a team meeting to change your culture. As important as team meetings may be, a multitude of other transactions are taking place on an everyday basis that you could potentially turn into an inspirational transaction. I mentioned in the very beginning of the book that these principles were more about character than process. Adjusting your lens to see through the eyes of inspiration is by far the most critical adjustment you will have to make.

Here's just a brief list of the possible inspirational transactions that could take place in the course of a day:

- When you answer the phone, do you sound like you're put off/out and disturbed when someone on your team calls you? Or do you sound inviting and interested?
- Make eye contact with people when you pass.
- Stay alert and listen in team meetings. You can always read e-mail when you get back to your desk rather than from your laptop during group discussions.
- When you greet people, take the initiative to learn about the other person first. Don't wait until they inquire about you to begin a dialogue.

There are hundreds of ways to create inspirational transactions that can ultimately be traced back to one of the seven principles. Make this a lifestyle and you will make inspiration contagious.

As a kid, I used to love to ride the Big Wheel at what was then Pontchartrain Beach in New Orleans. I'm sure you yourself have probably ridden on such an amusement park ride. The wheel begins to turn and you feel the centrifugal force pulling you up against the back wall of the wheel. That's exactly what happens when you begin to create a series of inspirational transactions and start living out these seven principles. Everyone around you, including customers, clients, contributors, and every other constituent group, gets pulled in to the force of inspiration.

I am often asked whose job it is, exactly, to create an inspiring culture. Without knowing anything about your role, your title, or your sphere of influence, I can unequivocally answer, "It's *your* job." Everyone can inspire someone today. No matter your personality. No matter your circumstances. In fact, I hope you've come to recognize that the more difficult your circumstances, the greater the opportunity for you to inspire others.

GET INSPIRED—CREATE A NEW CULTURE

Outcome Objectives for Week Twelve

- You will be able to clearly assess your existing culture as being one that is conducive for inspiring or one that needs changing.

- You will be able to identify a series of inspirational transactions that are within your realm of authority to implement.

Equipping Yourself

1. Based on your personality profile, what are your greatest leadership strengths? What negative tendencies do you need to watch out for and overcome?

2. How would you describe your company's culture as it currently exists?

3. What do you think it means to "create a culture of inspiration"? What might that look like?

4. What are some "inspiration busters" for you? Can you identify them for the people on your team and in your family? If so, what are they?

5. What is one thing you can do today to create more of an inspiring environment for people around you?

Inspiring Others

1. Lead a discussion with your team about what the key ingredients of Coach John Wooden's success were. How can these findings be incorporated into your culture as a company? How can your team in particular begin implementing these principles?

2. Know your people.

   • Take some time to think about each person on your team, and jot down each person's personality profile.

   • List the person's strengths and needs according to the profile's description, and keep that information close at hand for the next month to remind you what to expect from each person and to tailor your communication to be most effective.

GOING DEEPER

• Write out a twelve-week plan, following the steps in this book, to create a culture of inspiration for your team. Be sure to put the preparation phase for each exercise in the schedule to give people enough time to complete all of the exercises.

• How do you hope the twelve-week program you are undertaking will affect your team as a group? Each person on the team? You as the leader?

The Courage to Inspire

A hero is no braver than an ordinary man, but he is braver five minutes longer.
—Ralph Waldo Emerson, American philosopher, essayist, poet

IN 1924, BRITISH CLIMBER George Mallory was asked why he wanted to climb Mount Everest, the tallest and most daunting mountain in the world and which, at the time, had never been scaled. Mallory replied with eloquent simplicity, "Because it's there." In the past century, climbing the most treacherous peaks in the world has become an obsession for a few brave men and women. They don't climb for fame or fortune. They climb to challenge themselves to reach for more than they've ever achieved before, to push past the limits of physical and psychological endurance, to stare death in the face—and take another step.

At the young age of twenty-one, Stacy Allison caught the bug. On her first major climb, on Mount Huntington in Alaska, she was merely 200 feet from the summit when her partner's ice ax broke. They turned around, bro- kenhearted, but even more determined to reach the top of as many peaks as possible. Stacy reflected, "Our ability to respond positively to setbacks fuels our creativity and lays the foundation for future successes."

The next year, Stacy reached the top of Mount McKinley, the tallest mountain on the continent of North America, and she participated with a team of women who climbed 22,495-foot Ama Dablam in Nepal's Himalayan range.

These feats, though, were only preparation for the ultimate challenge: Mount Everest. She joined the North Face Expedition, but they failed to reach the top. Stacy and her fellow climbers were caught in the worst storm on the mountain in forty years, and they were trapped in a snow cave for five days at 23,500 feet. Again, she faced the reality of failure to attain a goal that had extracted a high price in time, effort, and money. Stacy learned a valuable lesson from this disappointment. "If you see yourself as trying to beat the mountain, eventually the mountain will win. You don't conquer mountains; you cooperate with them."

She returned to Mount Everest with a different team, the Northwest American Everest Expedition, and after climbing from base camp to base camp for twenty-nine days and a final push to the top, Stacy became the first American woman to reach the top of the world, at 29,028 feet.

Stacy has also led teams up the slopes of K2, thought by many to be the most difficult mountain in the world to climb. As a leader, she valued each person as much or more than the goal of reaching the summit. On one of these expeditions, for instance, three of the seven members of the team reached the top, but injury to one necessitated that the entire team call off the climb and head back down.

The few dedicated climbers who attempt the world's highest peaks endure grueling training and invest significant portions of their lives and finances to participate in an expedition. When they finally arrive in Nepal or Tibet, they don't get off the plane and hike to the top. They face weeks, if not months, of additional preparations, securing resources and assistance and setting up one base camp after another. The elevations are so difficult on the human body that climbers have to become acclimated to each camp for several days before they can make the next ascent.

The effort, expense, and tenacity pay off in stories of triumph and tragedy. Those who climb to the top of the world experience excruciating moments of self-doubt and conflict with team members about decisions made by oxygen-starved brains. Still, these men and women are driven to try to achieve what few others have dared. They know they may fail, but that doesn't stop them. In fact, nothing—except weather, injury, or death—will stop them. That's the essence of their courage.

The lessons Stacy Allison learned in climbing translate to every arena in life. Her two books, *Beyond the Limits: A Woman's Triumph on Everest* and *Many Mountains to Climb: Reflections on Competence, Courage, and Commitment*, recount her experiences in climbing the most perilous mountains in the world, and identify hard-earned principles for overcoming struggle applied to our daily lives. The difficulties we all face, she is certain, will make or break us. Reflecting on her role as a team builder, she writes: "In any endeavor, leaders should inspire members of the team with a passion for success, but within the framework of team effort. One of the most crucial things to realize, feel, and remember is that when one team member succeeds, the entire team succeeds."

The Challenge of Leadership

In the introduction, I promised that if you would work through even one of the seven principles in this book you would see very positive change. And it's true. Just one principle will, as I put it, "move the needle forward in your ability to inspire others." Of course, the more principles you work through, the more changes you can expect. But if you want to start small, and add more later, that's fine. The important thing is that you start— right where you are. Some of you will . . . but some of you won't.

When men and women in executive and management positions tell me, "I just can't inspire people," they've got it all wrong. No one is asking them to forsake their God-given personality to become something they're not. Instead, I'm asking them to become all they can be in relationships, to learn a few basic principles and apply them at work and at home. Can they do that? Of course they can. I know. I've witnessed it.

Some who read this book will embrace the seven principles, will bind the principles to them like glue, and will use them zealously to inspire to greatness everyone with whom they come in contact. Others will start out with the best of intentions—then drop the ball, as many people have done before them. Still others won't even try at all.

Why *do* some people rise to the challenge of inspiring others but some people don't? There may be a complicated matrix of reasons, but at the core it's not primarily a lack of experience, training, or personality—it's the lack of *courage*. Without courage, all the skills in the world are under-utilized. They lie dormant—because of fear.

Fears are validated by excuses. We tell ourselves that there are *good reasons* why we don't "reach out" and inspire someone. Here are just a few I've heard (some I've used myself) that attempt to validate resistance to change:

- "I'm too busy to think about it."
- "I'm under too much pressure from the boss to take time to learn 'inspiration principles.'"
- "Inspire people? It's just not me."
- "I'd like to spend time motivating my team, but they just don't respond to that kind of thing quickly enough."
- "My employees don't appreciate me. They're not worth it."
- "I'd come across as phony."
- "I don't want to expose myself to people any more than I have to."
- "I don't know how."
- "I'm confused."
- "I'm not a good speaker."
- "That's just too much to add to our team meeting. Our stockholders don't pay us to hold hands and feel good about ourselves."
- "If my boss knew I was spending time trying to inspire my team, I'd be fired today."

Excuses, excuses, and the one I've heard the most is the classic, "I don't want to look stupid."

Maybe you feel the same way. Perhaps stereotypes fill your mind. They are certainly a part of our lives. When we think of NFL quarterbacks, we think of Brett Favre, Tom Brady, or Peyton Manning. When we think of rich people, we think of Bill Gates and Warren Buffett. In the same way, when we think about inspiring people, we often think of high-profile, over-the-top people like Tony Robbins and Zig Ziglar. They're gifted and effective, true—but you don't have to receive a DNA transplant from one of these people to be an inspiring leader! And no one is asking you to become something you're not. Instead, I'm asking you to learn a few basic principles and to begin to apply them at work and at home to build an inspiring culture. Can you do that?

Of course you can. I've seen men and women muster the courage to take steps, one by one, to overcome their fear and create a culture of inspiration. In most cases, these steps were small, yet they produced major benefits. They'll do the same for you, but only to the same extent that your level of desperation surpasses your level of fear. Until then, you will cling to the familiar and forfeit the prospects of progress.

Next Steps

At some point, though, all of us need to step back, take a good look at our lives, and ask if we're valuing the right things. Do we live to avoid conflict? Do we value placating our boss more than caring for our team? Is self-protection our highest virtue? Or are we willing to call a spade a spade, step out, take a risk, and try to make a difference in someone's life?

You're willing to risk it, you say? Okay then; let's get started. Pick a principle—*any* principle. Here they are for your quick review.

1. Start being real—today! Take off your mask and be authentic—from now on!

2. Look around you. Who's got a dream? Connect with that individual—just him or her, to start—and watch the inspiration begin to swell.

3. Begin looking for someone's hidden abilities—I dare you! And when you notice them, name them and nurture them. That person will stand a little taller from this time forth.

4. Make a decision—*right now*—to be credible in every way. Shed any pretense and be honest at all times. People are inspired by those they can trust.

5. Tell a good story—this very night—to your tired spouse who's had a hard day, to a friend who's down in the dumps, or to your son who came home with two Ds on his report card. Do you have something to say that will inspire this loved one? I bet you do.

6. Pick someone—anyone—who needs help living life on *purpose*; then dedicate your time and energy to helping her find the purpose that she needs to live out.

7. Change your culture—beginning with you. Watch the words that come out of your mouth. If they are edifying and affirming, by all means, say them. But if they're just critical and condemning, bite your tongue. Do this a few times and it will become natural to let only the good come out. And when the good outweighs the bad, believe me, the climate will *change*.

That wasn't so hard, was it? Practicing just one principle is like throwing a rock into the center of a motionless lake. That rock (you!) will come in contact with one person . . . but it doesn't stop there. Watch for the ripple. It'll move outward toward shore. The person you influence will have an impact on others, but only if *you* make the first move.

Go ahead. Be the rock that starts the ripple effect—*today*.

When we finally get the courage to take steps forward, it is perhaps *we* who are most affected.

- As we help others identify their dreams, ours come into sharper focus.

- When we notice, name, and nurture others' abilities, we craft our leadership skills.

- As we try to enrich others with great stories and defining moments from our own lives, our lives become immeasurably richer because others tell us stories of failure and courage.

- Instead of the constant stress of trying to force people to be successful so we look good, we can relax, devote ourselves to helping them align their desires with the company's goals, and stand back and watch the powerfully positive chemical reaction.

- At the end of each day, we go home and build into our spouses and children in the same way, loving them, affirming them, listening to them, and helping them soar. And we sleep soundly, knowing our lives *really* matter.

GET INSPIRED—THE COURAGE TO INSPIRE

Outcome Objectives

- You will be able to share at least three life lessons from the life of Stacy Allison using the metaphor of mountain climbing.

- You will be able to recognize and effectively deal with people who are resistant to change.

- You will be able to write down and put into action at least three next steps for implementing the principles in this book.

Equipping Yourself

1. What does Stacy Allison's story teach us about goals, teamwork, setbacks, and accomplishments?

2. What are some fears and excuses that you've heard from people who didn't want to implement change? What are some you've used?

3. What are your expectations as you think of implementing the seven principles in this book? Do you expect instantaneous or gradual change to occur? Explain your answer.

4. What's the next step for you?

5. What difference will your implementation of these principles make in your team at work and in your family a month from now, six months from now, and a year from now?

Inspiring Others

1. Invite your team to participate in a discussion summarizing Stacy Allison's story. Ask the team members to identify and apply at least three insights from her story to your business challenges.

2. Introduce the concept of the twelve-week program to your team and listen to their reaction. What expectations do they have for the program?

    *   Tell the team what you hope to accomplish and how the exercises will change your organization and the work of the individuals.

    *   Outline the schedule for the program and introduce all the exercises to the team members so they will be prepared for each week's experience.

    *   Assign a different team member (or members) to be the inspiration leader for one of the weeks.

    *   Take note of positive and negative comments and work to address the negative comments.

GOING DEEPER

Plan a team retreat for a day. Invite each team member to select one of the seven principles expounded in this book and to facilitate a discussion around it. Also ask each person to choose one of the learning activities that corresponds to the principle they selected and lead the group through that action item.

Inspiration Blvd.
Personality Profile

THE INSPIRATION BLVD. Personality Profile contains twenty statements. Don't think too long or too hard about your answers. Indicate the answer that best fits your experiences. In some cases, two answers may seem equally true of you, but pick one. You'll probably find that you are a blend of a couple of the major profiles. The statements address four main areas: your motivations, needs, and desires in relationships; your stress responses; your leadership goals; and your communication style.

After you complete the scoring sheet, read the descriptions of the four profiles—Commander, Coach, Advocate, and Accountability Partner—in the section titled "Know Yourself, Be Yourself: Four Inspiring Personality Types" found in the chapter about Principle 1 (Be Authentic).

Circle the letter to indicate the response that best fits you.

1. I am most energized by:
    a. Discovering new ways to help people and achieve success
    b. Challenges
    c. Motivating others to succeed
    d. Systems and numbers that actually work

2. When tasks are given to me, I:
    a. Get going immediately
    b. Find the best system to do the job
    c. Think about the best and most creative way to accomplish the job
    d. Get others involved and discuss each person's role

3. To be most effective, I need:
    a. Individual attention and affirmation
    b. A creative, stress-free environment
    c. Plenty of authority and high goals
    d. Specific directions and control over the process

4. When I'm in a group, I:
    a. Am often very quiet
    b. Delight in meaningful conversations with a few people
    c. Enjoy telling and hearing great stories
    d. Am usually the center of attention

5. When I feel stressed, I:
    a. Become demanding and impatient
    b. Withdraw and focus on what I can control myself
    c. Get my feelings hurt and become confused and hesitant
    d. Feel hurt and become defiant

6. I work best in an environment that:
    a. Is friendly but has clear direction and expectations
    b. Gives me plenty of opportunity to take charge and generate action
    c. Allows me to influence others and build a team
    d. Provides plenty of time to think, plan, and discuss options

7. I feel most fulfilled when:
   a. A lot of people appreciate the impact I've had on them
   b. Others appreciate the new ideas I've offered
   c. I have accomplished goals nobody thought I could achieve
   d. I've checked off all of the boxes on my list

8. When a new idea is communicated:
   a. I need to know how it impacts what I'm already doing
   b. I'm ready to make it happen
   c. I carefully think about it to see if it makes sense and can be improved
   d. I feel thrilled if it was my idea and discouraged if it wasn't

9. When people ask for my opinion:
   a. I'm absolutely sure I'm right
   b. I ask a question to clarify what is wanted
   c. I give it, often without thinking before I speak
   d. I let others answer while I analyze the question and consider my response

10. The influence I want to have on others is to:
    a. Encourage them to find new, creative ways to succeed
    b. Provide accurate data in a timely manner for them
    c. Challenge their socks off
    d. Motivate them to succeed individually and as a team

11. People see me as:
    a. Disciplined, consistent, and efficient, but sometimes aloof
    b. Warm, fun, and verbal, but sometimes off track
    c. Kind, reflective, and patient, but sometimes fragile
    d. Direct, intense, and driven, but sometimes impatient

12. When people who report to me struggle or fail, I:
    a. Kick them in the butt to get them back on track
    b. Try to help them understand what went wrong so they can make adjustments
    c. Become their best cheerleader
    d. Do it myself next time

13. To help others make decisions, I:
    a. Provide plenty of accurate information for them
    b. Ask questions to help them discover the best path
    c. Make the decision for them if they take too long
    d. Encourage them to do what I think they should do

14. When people who report to me succeed, I:
    a. Throw a party!
    b. Give them even bigger challenges as a reward
    c. Offer heartfelt congratulations
    d. Am happy for them, but to be honest, I wonder how they did it, because they didn't seem to know what they were doing

15. The kind of direction I give is:
    a. Clear, quick, and practical
    b. Personal and encouraging
    c. Precise with deadlines
    d. Thoughtful, patient, and open to other options

16. When someone is unresponsive to my leadership, I often:
    a. Feel hurt and confront the person personally
    b. Feel tense and go back to what I can control
    c. Feel confused and analyze the situation
    d. Feel angry and demand a response

17. I feel like quitting when:
    a. Nobody appreciates me
    b. I feel pressure to make snap decisions and do meaningless tasks
    c. Hell freezes over (I can always figure out a solution)
    d. Expectations aren't clear and deadlines aren't enforced

18. My verbal skills are:
    a. Controlled and cautious
    b. Strong and direct
    c. Positive and personal
    d. Warm, relaxed, and interactive

19. When I think I'm being treated unfairly, I:
    a. Insist that systems and rules be followed
    b. Enlist others to be on my side
    c. Feel very discouraged and hopeless
    d. Become furious and impatient

20. The people I've led for an extended time would say I'm:
    a. A bold visionary
    b. A great friend
    c. Very dependable
    d. Their greatest fan

Scoring

Circle the responses you indicated for each statement, and tally the number of circled letters in each column.

	Commander	Coach	Advocate	Accountability Partner
1.	B	C	A	D
2.	A	D	C	B
3.	C	A	B	D
4.	D	B	C	A
5.	A	D	C	B
6.	B	C	D	A
7.	C	A	B	D
8.	B	D	C	A
9.	A	C	D	B
10.	C	D	A	B
11.	D	B	C	A
12.	A	C	B	D
13.	C	D	B	A
14.	B	A	C	D
15.	A	B	D	C
16.	D	A	C	B
17.	C	A	B	D
18.	B	C	D	A
19.	D	B	C	A
20.	A	D	B	C
	_____	_____	_____	_____

Review and Application

If one of the columns has a score of 12 or more, you have a fairly clear inspiration personality profile. And if two of the columns have a combined score of 15 or more, but neither column is more than 10, you are a strong blend of these two.

Inspiration Blvd. 360 Profile

THIS TOOL IS designed to give people accurate and comprehensive feedback from those who know them best. Many managers use the 360 Profile to gather perceptions and offer insights to those who report to them, but individuals can also take the initiative to gather feedback from coworkers, family members, and friends.

If you are orchestrating the profile to get feedback on yourself, here's how it works:

> Select someone—a professional coach, mentor, or supervisor—to help you choose the people who will be involved. Later, this person will also help you interpret and apply the results.

> Go online to www.inspirationblvd.com to set up the 360 Profile. On the site, list the names of your coach (or supervisor, if that person is going to coordinate the profile for you) and the nine other participants (described in the next step in this list). Make sure to write down the password that people will use to fill out the inventory on you.

Ask the ten people you selected to take about twenty minutes to go online and fill out the inventory with you in mind. These ten people should include:

- Your direct supervisor or director
- Four peers
- Three family members
- Two friends

Instruct these people to go to www.inspirationblvd.com and click on "360 Profile." They will type in your name, their name, and the password, and then complete the inventory about you. Give them a deadline that you and your mentor will determine—probably no longer than two weeks away. Explain that their answers will be compiled for a report and will be kept strictly confidential.

After a week, go online to see who has not yet completed the profile. Send a reminder to those participants.

When everyone has completed the profile, we will send a report to your coach or mentor. Set aside at least two hours to go over the results with him or her.

If you are a team member rather than a manager, you can still use the 360 Profile. Simply follow the steps above for each team member, and list yourself as the coach and the direct supervisor.

The 360 Profile contains three sections. As you complete each one, click "Next" to go to the next one.

For items 1–20, use this scale:

5   Always

4   Often

4   Sometimes

2   Seldom

1   Never

0   N/A

Section 1

CHARACTER TRAITS

1. Consistently honest and trustworthy

2. Accepts constructive criticism with poise

3. Has an infectious, optimistic attitude

4. Rigorously objective about opportunities and problems

5. Punctual and prompt to complete assignments

SKILLS

6. Eager to learn new skills

7. Efficient and effective

8. Prioritizes responsibilities

9. Effective in leading others

10. Committed to excellence

TEAMWORK

11. Works with others to find common ground to solve problems

12. Listens well and asks good questions

13. Has realistic expectations of self and others

14. Delegates with clear expectations

15. Gladly celebrates others' successes

RESOLVING CONFLICT

16. Responds to authority with appropriate respect

17. Communicates clearly under stress

18. In tense situations with others, first tries to understand the other person's point of view

19. Anticipates problems before they arise

20. Doesn't hold grudges or take revenge

Section 2

Rate each of these qualities on a scale of 0 (a big problem) to 10 (a great strength).

Loyal	0 1 2 3 4 5 6 7 8 9 10
Enthusiastic	0 1 2 3 4 5 6 7 8 9 10
Helps others uncover dreams and abilities	0 1 2 3 4 5 6 7 8 9 10
Visionary	0 1 2 3 4 5 6 7 8 9 10
Detailed	0 1 2 3 4 5 6 7 8 9 10
Trustworthy	0 1 2 3 4 5 6 7 8 9 10
Builds a team	0 1 2 3 4 5 6 7 8 9 10
Inspiring	0 1 2 3 4 5 6 7 8 9 10
Analytical	0 1 2 3 4 5 6 7 8 9 10
Tells great stories	0 1 2 3 4 5 6 7 8 9 10

Section 3

Answer each of the following questions as clearly and honestly as possible. Remember, your answers will be kept confidential. A report that lists all of your responses for each question will be provided to the person being profiled. Please write one to four sentences for each question.

- What exceptional character qualities, skills, and abilities have you seen in this person? (What traits can you easily notice, name, and nurture?)

- In what relationships (at work or at home) does this person have the most positive influence?

- What are this person's passions? What causes his or her eyes to light up?

- What relationships and recurring situations cause him or her to lose focus, energy, and enthusiasm?

- What can you imagine might be this person's highest and best impact a year from now? Five years from now?

Four People Who Inspired Others

Winston Churchill

Winston's father, Lord Randolph Churchill, sent him off to boarding school and wrote his son scathing letters describing his disappointment in him. His socialite mother neglected him because she was preoccupied with her many lovers, including the Duke of Windsor. In his early life, the only person who genuinely cared for Winston was his nanny.

In the army, young Winston was determined to prove himself, both as a soldier and as a correspondent in India and in the Boer War in South Africa. Soon, though, the lure of politics led him to run for Parliament, and he was elected as one of its youngest members.

Winston suffered a major professional setback, however, when he was blamed for the disastrous strategy of invading Turkey. He resigned his war cabinet post and returned to the infantry in France.

Other milestones in Churchill's life included:

- He became Chancellor of the Exchequer, one step away from being prime minister.
- After the crisis over Irish independence, he resigned his role again and became a backbencher in Parliament. Most considered his political career to be over.
- After Adolf Hitler became chancellor of Germany in 1933, Churchill founded and led a growing movement called "Arms and the Covenant" to rearm England for the war he was certain would come; this movement soon became an object of public scorn.
- He became so depressed it was difficult for him to function.
- He had accumulated massive personal debt and was broke; he asked a businessman, Bernard Baruch, for a job in the business world.
- Five people (his wife, Baruch, and three members of Parliament) stepped up and expressed their strong belief in Churchill's ability to still have impact as a political leader.
- Four hard years later, Churchill became prime minister of England.
- He led England through what he called "our finest hour" of defying Hitler. The people's faith in Churchill made all the difference.

BUILDING YOUR STORY

- How can you compare the cultural and political times of Winston Churchill to our own world?
- What metaphor (or metaphors) can you pull from Churchill's story that illustrates something about the world of business you work in?
- What life lessons can you learn from Churchill's life and apply to your life as a leader?

Mel Fisher

On July 20, 1985, Mel Fisher stood on the deck of his salvage boat off the Florida Keys. He and his crew were going through the same routine they'd done a thousand times before. For seventeen years, Fisher had been looking for *Nuestra Señora de Atocha*, a Spanish galleon that sank in a hurricane in 1622. The ship's manifest in Madrid described an almost unimaginable treasure—gold, silver, and emeralds—so valuable that the Spanish empire went into an economic depression when the news of the *Atocha's* sinking was announced in court.

Milestones in Mel Fisher's journey included:

- A diving accident claimed the lives of his son and daughter-in-law.

- He ran out of money numerous times and had to continue to find investors who believed in his dream.

- He knew he was close to his goal several times by finding items that were undoubtedly from the *Atocha*.

- On July 19, 1985, people in Key West said Mel Fisher was a fool.

- On July 20, 1985, people around the world hailed Fisher as a genius.

- The treasure he found on that hot day in July yielded a stack of gold and silver bars six feet high, eight feet wide, and forty feet long.

- The estimated value of Fisher's treasure trove was more than $400 million.

BUILDING YOUR STORY

- Using "treasure hunt" as a metaphor, how would you relate this to both your personal pursuits and your professional pursuits?

- What life lessons can you learn from Mel Fisher's story that you could apply to yourself, your team, and your organization?

Queen Elizabeth I

If anyone ever had a reason to use her family background as an excuse for self-pity and passivity, Elizabeth did. She grew up in one of the most tumultuous, bitter families known to history. Her father, Henry VIII of England, had discarded each of his wives, one by one, when she failed to produce male heirs. His first wife, Catherine of Aragon, gave him only a daughter, Mary. Henry demanded a divorce. When the Catholic Church told him no, he chose an archbishop who would grant the divorce and then founded his own church, the Church of England—of which he conveniently declared himself to be the head.

After the divorce, the woman of his dreams, Anne Boleyn, became pregnant, and Henry was sure he finally had an heir. Anne, though, gave the disappointed king another girl—Elizabeth. Anne was unable to have another child, so Henry had her beheaded when Elizabeth was just three years old. Henry declared Elizabeth illegitimate.

Other milestones in Elizabeth's life included:

- Her father Henry VIII married four more times in pursuit of a son.

- After Henry's death, his son, Edward, became king, bypassing Mary's and Elizabeth's (his older half-sisters) claims to the throne.

- Upon Edward's death, Elizabeth's half sister, Mary, took the throne. During her reign, Mary earned the nickname "Bloody Mary" because of her cruelty to anyone who didn't support her cause.

- Mary accused Elizabeth of supporting Protestants and had her imprisoned.

- Elizabeth used her years in prison to study and train for the day when she herself might come to power

- Her country was on the brink of civil war when she took the throne.

- Her reign—the Elizabethan Age—saw the remarkable achievements of William Shakespeare, Isaac Newton, Walter Raleigh, and Francis Drake, among other notable minds.

- Though Elizabeth lived four centuries before women's rights, she exemplified leadership on the grandest scale. One of her most famous quotes to that effect is, "I know I have the body of a weak and feeble woman, but I have the heart and stomach of a king."

BUILDING YOUR STORY

- How can you relate Elizabeth's personal and cultural circumstances to where you live or where you work today?
- How would you describe Elizabeth's attitude toward personal setbacks and personal injustices?
- What life lessons can you learn from the story of Elizabeth that you could apply to your personal life? Your professional life?

Robert E. Lee

In the fall of 1865, students at the struggling Washington College in Lexington, Virginia, watched their new president actively structure a new academic curriculum. Though his involvement with this endeavor was full-on, he moved very slowly around the campus, whether on his majestic gray horse or on foot. He also looked very, very old. And yet . . . this man was perhaps the most highly respected person on both sides of the recently reunited nation.

Four and a half years earlier, Robert E. Lee had been a colonel in the United States Army. As Southern states seceded from the Union, the army's commanding officer, General Winfield Scott, called Lee to Washington. There, Lincoln offered him command of Union forces for the imminent Civil War. In subsequent days at his home across the Potomac River in Arlington, Virginia, Lee wrestled with his decision. He was against secession, and he had left directions in his will to free all the slaves he and his wife had inherited from her father. Having graduated with highest honors from West Point, he had served his country with honor during the Mexican War and in the peace that followed. But when Virginia left the

Union, Lee determined not to draw his sword against his native state. He graciously declined Lincoln's offer.

Other milestones in the life of Robert E. Lee include:

- He volunteered to serve in the Virginia militia and eventually became Confederate President Jefferson Davis's military aide.

- When Lee was eventually given command of all the Confederate Army, Union General George B. McClellan assumed Lee would prove to be too timid in the field because of his gentle and warm personality.

- Over the next three years, however, Lee won time and time again even though his army was outmanned, outgunned, underfed, and poorly clothed.

- Lee's men respected him as a deeply spiritual man.

- In April 1865, military brilliance couldn't overcome the lack of men, gunpowder, and food; Lee surrendered to General Ulysses S. Grant at Appomattox Court House.

- After the war, an insurance company offered Lee a salary of $50,000 a year for the use of his name. Lee responded by saying, "Don't you think that if my name is worth $50,000 a year, I ought to be very careful about taking care of it?"

- Instead, he accepted the offer to become president of bankrupt Washington College for a salary of $1,500 a year because he wanted to help young men get a good education.

- Lee is credited by many historians as being the most influential postwar voice of reconciliation and healing in the south.

BUILDING YOUR STORY

- In what ways are your culture and these times similar to that of Robert E. Lee's?

- Why did General McClellan assume that Lee would be timid in the battlefield? How would you relate that to some of the personality types you learned about in this book?

- Why was it so important to Lee not to let an insurance company "use his name"? How might Lee's response help us both personally and professionally as we think about protecting our own name?
- How can you relate and apply Lee's role as a voice of reconciliation to the world in which you live and work?
- What other life lessons can you find and apply from the life of Robert E. Lee?

ABOUT THE AUTHOR

TERRY BARBER is the "chief inspirator" for Grizzard Communications Group, primarily serving the nonprofit health care segment, as well as colleges and universities, in the area of philanthropic branding. Some of the organizations with which he consults include Johns Hopkins Sidney Kimmel Cancer Center, Duke Cancer Center, Cedars-Sinai Hospital, and the Huntsman Cancer Center of Salt Lake City, Utah.

Terry is a popular speaker for corporate training and events and an inspirational resource to the nonprofit community. He has been interviewed on ABC News Now, Fox News, and CNN Radio, and featured in *Forbes*, *BusinessWeek*, the American Management Association, and on HR.com. Additionally, he speaks somewhere in the United States each week on "How to Create an Inspiring Culture."

In the fall of 1987, Terry started and managed a nonprofit company that focused on helping teens develop positive, principle-based self-esteem. This provided the opportunity to serve literally hundreds of schools nationwide and to personally speak to more than five hundred thousand of these students in assembly and classroom settings. He has also written and produced a six-part video curriculum on the same topic that has been used in more than six hundred school districts around the United States.

Most recently, Terry created a Web 2.0 initiative called Inspiration Blvd., LLC (www.inspirationblvd.com), where he holds the title of "chief inspirational officer." The website is capturing the attention and imagination of people interested both in inspiring others and in being inspired.

Terry holds a masters degree from New Orleans Baptist Seminary. He continues to be actively involved in his passion for an orphanage in Uganda and child sponsorship and early childhood education in Guatemala.

He resides in Alpharetta, Georgia, and is married to Debbi. He is proud of his four daughters and three grandchildren.

ABOUT INSPIRATION BLVD.

FOR THOSE WHO aspire to work and live in a culture of inspiration,

- where encouragement is the norm,
- where affirmation is authentic,
- where aspiration is applauded,

InspirationBlvd.com is the ultimate resource.

Here are some offerings from Terry Barber and InspirationBlvd.com:

Train Others Workshop—No one from the outside can have the same impact and influence on the organization you serve as you do. Inspiration Blvd. LLC hosts training workshops each month so you can teach and train others to use the principles found in this book. Check www.inspirationblvd.com for the workshop nearest you.

Corporate Parables Workshop—Learn to be an effective communicator of stories that teach. Your team meetings will never be the same, and corporate gatherings will come alive. This is a great opportunity to tap into the many stories that are lying dormant within your organization. This workshop is high energy and a fun, powerful way to raise the inspiration factor in your company or organization.

Lunch and Learns—Serve up inspiration at lunch. We will present a compressed, substantive, and entertaining session on any one of the seven principles presented in *The Inspiration Factor.*

Leadership Retreats—For a transformational experience, set aside 1.5 days with executives and team leaders to focus on integrating the seven principles of *The Inspiration Factor.* This is an environment that is low on lecture and high on involvement.

www.inspirationblvd.com
Twitter: @inspirationblvd
Email: info@inspirationblvd.com
Blog: www.inspirationfactor.wordpress.com

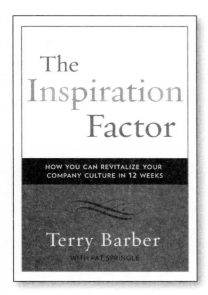

ORDER MORE BOOKS

To order more books and learn about discount and shipping information go to

www.inspirationblvd.com.